LASER-SHARP
FOCUS

A NO-FLUFF GUIDE TO IMPROVED CONCENTRATION, MAXIMISED PRODUCTIVITY AND FAST-TRACK TO SUCCESS

JOANNA JAST

First Print Edition 2016

ISBN: 978-0-473-34933-2

DISCLAIMER

The information in this book is intended for educational and informational purposes only and should not be taken as expert instructions or commands. It should not be treated as advice or as a substitute for seeking help from an appropriately trained health professional or expert. While all attempts have been made to verify the information provided in this book at the time of writing, the author and publisher do not assume any responsibility for errors, omissions, or contrary interpretations of the subject matter herein. The author and publisher therefore disclaim any liability to any party for any loss, damage, or disruption caused by errors or omissions, whether such errors or omissions result from negligence, accident, or other cause. Adherence to all applicable laws and regulations, including international, national, federal, local, professional licencing, business practices, educational advertising and all other aspects of doing business under any jurisdiction is the sole responsibility of the purchaser or the reader.

Neither the author nor the publisher assumes any responsibility or liability whatsoever on behalf of the purchaser or reader of these materials.

Any perceived slight of any individual or organisation is purely unintentional. Names and characters of the persons presented in the book have been changed to protect their privacy.

YOUR FREE GIFT

Thank you for choosing *Laser-Sharp Focus*. A No-Fluff Guide to Improved Concentration, Maximised Productivity and Fast-Track to Success.

To help you put the advice presented in this book into practice, I've created a Quick Action Guide.

Head to: http://www.theshapeshiftersclub.com/lsf-quickactionguide to **download** the guide **now**.

CONTENTS

INTRODUCTION

'Even brief mental blocks created by shifting between tasks can cost as much as 40% of someone's productive time.'[1]

How much of your time do you spend unfocused? How much of your time can you *afford* to spend unfocused?

How much more could you achieve, do, earn? How much time could you have left to enjoy life?

Take a moment to let that sink in.

The modern reality is unfocused. Always on-line, multitasking galore, chasing the next shiny thing, battling with information overload.

You know it's not good for you—your wellbeing and your success suffer because of it. So you search for ways to improve your focus and boost your mental powers. But there is so much information out there it makes you dizzy. You run from one approach to another, increasingly confused and frustrated. You waste even more time on trying strategies that don't work for you, make things worse, or don't fit with your situation. So you procrastinate even more, or worse—give up completely and stay stuck.

Finding that perfect way to focus can be frustrating and time consuming. It took me a good few years to figure out what worked for me, and I am still tweaking my system as I go.

We are all different and our needs change as we go through life. Our approach to make our minds work should also adapt to our needs. But more often than not, this is not the case.

Much of the advice on improving your 'mental powers' that's out there doesn't help either. It is generic and superficial, and definitely does not take into consideration your specific needs at the time.

This book will change the way you try to focus on the job-at-hand. Whether you're a complete beginner, or someone who has tried and failed a few times, you will find tips and tricks to help you boost your ability to concentrate.

In this book, I am going to show you:

- How to identify what specifically is not working within your current 'focus system.'
- Specific strategies you can use to eliminate procrastination, minimize distractions, avoid interruptions, keep your mind on track, your emotions under control, and your body at top-level performance.
- Guidelines to create a system that can adapt to your changing needs so that you focus on your job, whatever it is, whenever you need to and wherever you are.

The content is organised in a step-by-step way to help you create a fail-proof system, allowing you to address all the important elements in a logical and helpful order.

Moreover, this approach, unlike many others, also recognises and takes into consideration your individual situation, providing you with a roadmap so that you can check where you are and what you need to do to get where you want to be. This system will grow with you.

This book is for people who:

- Struggle with distractions and interruptions
- Are consumed by procrastination

- Try and fail to constantly 'motivate themselves'
- Suffer from 'wandering mind'
- Feel they are not as productive as they could be

If any of the above describes you, keep reading—this book will show you how to tackle these problems, sharpen your focus, get things done, achieve your goals faster, and have time to enjoy life.

How do I know?

I'm a life-long learner, a teacher/trainer, doctor and author/blogger with passion for discovering how our minds and human behaviour work.

I have researched the best strategies, supported by scientific evidence, and tried every single one of them. These strategies helped me to go from being a very average, and at times struggling, student, to acing exams, mastering two foreign languages, gaining a few more qualifications, and successfully juggling multiple jobs and other commitments simultaneously.

I have shared my ideas and this very system with many people around the world through my online courses, Quora answers, blog posts and personal advice, showing strategies that actually made a difference to people's productivity and lives.

I sifted through hundreds of books, articles and sometimes incredibly boring scientific papers on the subjects of focus, concentration, productivity, habits and other 'brain powers,' and distilled what's out there into an easy-to-read, simple-to-follow system that can be personalised. No-nonsense, no 'inspirational' fluff and no snake-oil.

By following this system, I developed an ability to sit down and 'snap into focus,' getting on with my tasks without fuss, completing them faster and with fewer errors, and having more time to enjoy life.

If you follow my system, you will be able to maximise your productivity, get your work done on time, achieve more and reach success faster. As a result, you'll spend less time at your desk or computer, and you'll have evenings, weekends and holidays to yourself. You'll have more time for your family and friends, and simply to enjoy your life and be happy.

So don't procrastinate any more. Don't 'think about it later.' Take action NOW.

Start your journey to laser-sharp focus, better concentration and maximised productivity today.

The strategies and techniques you're about to read have helped me, and many other people create positive, lasting changes in their work, studies and personal lives.

All you need to do is to keep reading, and the strategies in this book will help you fast-track your success—at work, in education and life.

WHAT THIS BOOK IS, AND WHAT IT'S NOT

Let me start with what this book is not, so that if you're looking for any of these, you can stop reading right now.

First of all, this book is NOT about ADHD/ADD (Attention Deficit Hyperactivity Disorder/Attention Deficit Disorder). If you have or suspect you may have ADHD or ADD, seek help from an appropriately qualified professional.

If you are struggling with concentration, attention, memory and/or any other cognitive problems because you have or suspect you may have a physical or mental health problem, seek help from your healthcare provider. You may still benefit from advice given in this book, once you've addressed the underlying problem, but please deal with your health appropriately.

This book does not deal with nootropics, 'brain stimulation devices,' or any other 'cognitive enhancers.' It does not cover anything that has been disproved by science or has 'inconclusive evidence' behind it.

This book is definitely NOT an inspirational book. You will not find any motivational quotes or advice 'how to motivate yourself to focus' here. I included a chapter on improving your motivation, but you need to have at least some motivation in the first place.

If your main problem is lack of motivation to do your job, study or attend to any other commitments/duties you have in life, you may benefit from the advice in this book. However, it may not be enough, or what you are in fact looking for. Get your motivation sorted first and foremost, and you can then return to this book and check if you still need advice on focusing.

This book is about focus as mental exercise: your ability to direct your attention, concentrate and sustain your mental efforts on whatever you're working (studying, reading, writing, etc.) at the time. This is not about finding focus, purpose, mission, passion, etc., in life, or finding focus for your business, career, creative endeavours, etc.

There are many books that deal with those topics, but this is not the one.

Advice you find in this book is not rocket science, but it is backed by science (cognitive neuroscience, educational theory and empirical or scientific evidence) and implementing it will help you become a 'rocket scientist' (if that's what's you're working toward). It is my personal system built on evidence-based practices and years of experience. I am sharing all this with you in the hope that you can benefit from my experience, too. However, be mindful that we are all individuals and not everything will work for everyone; what's worked for me may not work for you. But the bottom line is: even the best advice in the world will not do anything for you if you don't put it into practice.

If you're an avid reader of self-help books and articles, an experienced student or a productivity fan, you may find nothing new here. Yes, to some extent this book is a re-hash of well-known stuff, but it is a well-organised rehash, and—unlike most other books of this type—easily adaptable to your personal, specific situation. I also packed it with lots of practical steps and examples on how to implement it in your life.

Whether you're a student struggling to focus on your coursework, a stay-at-home mum trying to set up a business, an entrepreneur, a freelance writer or an office worker looking to boost your productivity, you will find this book helpful. If you want to be able to focus on the job at hand instantaneously and stay on the task until you finish it (or however long you can afford), this book is for you. If you're looking for a well-proven system, keep reading. But most of all, if you're disappointed with blanket, cure-all strategies, 'focus boosting' music/apps/other magical devices, can't digest boring and heavy scientific reads, but don't like fluffy, padded-out books—this is a must-read for you.

Easy-to-read, concise, jam-packed with practical steps that can be adjusted to your specific problems—here is my Laser-Sharp Focus system for you, written to help you succeed—faster.

HOW TO READ THIS BOOK

This book has been organised in a way that follows so called 'logical sequence of events;' that is, starting from the beginning and gradually working through the next steps.

Why?

Because we need to learn to crawl first before we attempt to walk, before we can run. Right?

Right.

And this book acknowledges there is a natural sequence of steps.

But...

On the other hand, if you're not a beginner, you won't need to start from crawling. If your legs were in a plaster cast for a long time or if you've just got your first-ever high heels, you will have different 'learn-to-walk' needs. Right?

Right.

That's why I have included The Focus Roadmap right at the beginning of the book: so that you can identify where you are now, look up where you want to go, and then find what steps you need to follow to quickly get to your goals.

Makes sense?

I hope so.

You can read this book from cover to cover in the order it is presented, or use the Roadmap and jump to the chapters that are of interest to you at this time. Either way, you will get specific advice on developing and maintaining a laser-sharp focus throughout your life.

But we are all different and we struggle to focus because of different problems.

Your struggles will not only differ from mine, but also change as you go through life, or even be different in different areas of life at the same time.

This is why I designed this book to guide you through your own situation or challenges.

In order to address your specific problems, you need to know what's working and what's not. If you already know—just skip to the parts or chapters of the book that may be of use to you.

If you don't know or would like to have a better understanding, I urge you to go to Chapter 2 and do the exercises included there. These tasks will help you identify your specific struggles. Once you've got clarity around that, look at the Roadmap to see where you can find useful info on how to address your specific problems.

And as you improve your focus and then work on maintaining it, life may throw you new challenges and you may find yourself struggling again, maybe even with different things. Use the Roadmap included in Chapter 2 to navigate the content provided in this book so you can always stay focused, no matter what your difficulty, age and state of mind is.

Whichever way you choose, keep reading.

PART 1 -

FIRST THINGS FIRST

CHAPTER I -
WHAT IS "FOCUS"
AND HOW DOES IT WORK?

Focus has many meanings depending on the context, but they all revolve around the state of clarity, a point of convergence, a centre of interest or activity.

Mental focus, which is what this book is about, refers to our ability to concentrate and direct our attention and energy onto something.

This definition implies that focus is a deliberate action. It is not a state of mind, at least not initially, and requires an active approach to bring our attention to what we want to focus on and then to maintain it.

That's good and bad news. It's bad for those of you who were hoping for some 'holy grail' of 'instant focus once and forever,' but good news for those of you frustrated with pursuing those elusive holy grails.

For simplicity, I use three terms, focus, attention, and concentration, almost interchangeably through this book. But, for the record, here is a very brief outline of the differences between them:

- Attention is your ability to attend to inside or outside stimuli; attention can be focused or divided
- Focus is your ability to direct your attention to one selected stimulus
- Concentration is your ability to sustain focus on one thing (stimulus) for a prolonged period of time [1]

There is no 'holy grail' of laser-sharp focus. There is no 'one size fits all,' either. The ability to focus is a skill you can learn, improve, and adapt to whatever your current needs are. How you achieve it depends on your individual situation, your mind-set, your skills and most of all your environment.

So stop chasing those holy grails and keep reading.

How Focus Works

Let's start with understanding how focus works and what can get in the way of your concentration.

Focus, as explained in the previous section, is your ability to direct your attention onto one thing (stimulus).

In a (simplified) nutshell we can say that attention (and hence focus) can be directed in **two ways: 'automatic' and 'intentional.'**

'Automatic attention' is very short-lived (8-12 seconds). It's geared up to detect danger in our environment—to hear, see, smell, or otherwise perceive any changes around and inside us. So any unexpected noise, flashes of light, stab in the back, pain in the stomach, or that fear rising in your head, will be automatically brought to your attention, dragging your focus away from whatever you're doing at the time.

Automatic attention evolved as a life-saving ability. However, in the modern day when every electronic device is equipped with flashing lights and a variety of annoying sounds, automatic attention can ruin your focus very quickly.

'Intentional attention' is subject to our conscious control. We turn it on when we want to focus on something, and off when no longer interested. Its natural span is... 10 minutes [2]. Not much, is it?

No, not enough to read a chapter, or definitely too little to complete a report.

Fortunately, we all have the ability to extend it beyond those meagre 10 minutes. But unless you put in extra effort to keep at it, your focus will start drifting away.

How can you do it?

To keep intentional focus on a target for longer than those 10 minutes, you need to feel involved in the task and find it attractive enough to keep going. These two factors can be influenced consciously and we will talk about it more in *Chapter 10: Problem with Attention Span? No Problem.*

However, being able to focus for longer periods of time is not just a matter of some attention superpower. Your body needs to feel comfortable enough to maintain its position, your mind has to be clear enough to follow the content, and your environment should not get in the way.

In this brief chapter I explained the key concepts that will be used throughout this book: attention, concentration and focus, and how they work. In the next chapter I will show you how to identify the problems with your focus.

CHAPTER 2 -
YOUR SPECIFIC SITUATION AND HOW TO
DIAGNOSE PROBLEMS IN YOUR SYSTEM

In this chapter we will talk about the very first steps you need to take in order to successfully improve your focus:

- Two types of problem with focus
- How to identify what's not working for you
- Identifying patterns
- Where to find useful advice on addressing your specific problems

The reason I started writing about focus and came up with the idea of my free 4-part email course 'Improve Your Focus' (parts of which have been incorporated into this book), was the frustration with blanket, 'cure-all' advice I came across on the Web.

A number of people I spoke to before writing this book: students, small business owners, entrepreneurs, wannabe-preneurs and career shifters, complained about their disillusionment with generic advice, ineffective techniques, and overall lack of practical 'how-to' they have encountered when seeking solutions to their focus problems.

Those of you who read my Quora answers or Shapeshifters Club blog posts may know about my particular view on meditation as a way to improve concentration.

Not that I have anything against meditation in general—it is a great way to enhance your physical and mental wellbeing, achieve focus, peace of mind, fulfilment, and other things. But it is not the only way to achieve those goals and may not work for everyone, and most of all it is not a 'cure-all'.

Do you know that failure to recognise what's not working (diagnostic errors) are the most common, costliest, and most dangerous medical mistakes? [1]

Luckily, our lives and health are not at risk here. Nevertheless, before you start investing time, effort and maybe even money (productivity apps, anyone?) into fixing your struggling concentration, take time to diagnose what's not working.

Diagnostic process is not used only in health settings. Understanding the problems first so that you can apply a targeted solution is the foundation of effective problem-solving strategies, regardless of the industry, specialty or areas of life.

I believe that if something is not working, the best way to fix it is to understand what's not working in the first place. This stems from my medical training: a good doctor will take time to understand the underlying cause of your illness before they prescribe any treatment. They will keep multiple hypotheses in mind, aware that different problems may present with similar symptoms. So he/she will explore the symptoms, run some tests, or do an x-ray.

Sadly, I am unable to diagnose your focus problems individually, but I have come up with a way to help you identify what's not working.

The section below will guide you through the process I use and recommend to many of my students. It may feel like it's time consuming and unnecessarily slowing the process, but it is worth the investment. I encourage you to run those logs for at least a few days, even if you feel you know what's not working for you.

Once you have completed your Distraction Logs, check the Laser Sharp Focus Roadmap at the end of this chapter for further suggestions regarding where to seek help specific to your problem(s).

TWO TYPES OF PROBLEMS WITH FOCUS

Now that you know how attention and focus work, you can imagine what may get in the way of you being focused.

Generally speaking, there are two types of focus problems:

- Threats to your **'Automatic attention,'** so anything your brain may perceive as potential danger and hence demand you refocus your attention onto it. Typically, these will be all types of distractions and interruptions, such as flashing lights, warning sounds and anything making a sudden appearance, noise, smell, etc.
- Threats to your **'Intentional Attention,'** that is, threats to your ability to focus for longer than those 10 minutes. Since this type of attention relies on your interest and comfort, anything that makes you feel uncomfortable, as well as boredom and lack of motivation, are likely to drive your focus away from your task. Usually, these problems manifest themselves as procrastination or distractions.

As you probably noticed, any of these problems can come from anywhere inside **your body, your mind** or **your** immediate **environment.** That's why Part 2 of this book is organised around the **three main 'focus danger zones:' your environment, your body and your mind.**

Usually, you are likely to experience more than one problem and often from more than one 'zone.' If you happen to have noisy neighbours whose arguments you can hear even with your windows closed, your mind will be tuning in and out of their arguments, e.g. out of curiosity or emotional arousal because you will be growing angry or frightened (if it is a really feisty fight). As a result, you may end up with a headache, which will add to your difficulties concentrating on your jobs.

Many people are able to identify a pattern or patterns to their struggles to focus. For instance, early in my journey to laser-sharp focus, my main problem was falling asleep when trying to study. More recently, when going through a period of personal crisis, I had to deal with my distracting thoughts about the situation. For you, it may be the flashing Facebook notification icon, or the chatter of the TV in the living room next door, which in turn makes you wonder what your friends have been up to or what's on the telly. Or your inner critic, who is never satisfied with the quality of work you produce.

HOW TO IDENTIFY WHAT'S NOT WORKING

The best way to identify what affects your ability to focus is to keep a **distraction log.** Distraction logs are simple data collection tools. All you need to do is to record every instance your focus drifted away from what you should be doing.

How do you do it?

It's really simple. Every time you get distracted from your task, pause to identify the cause. Is it something in **your environment** that dragged your attention away from your job at hand? Or is it something happening with **your body?** Or maybe it's your thoughts, or emotions or anything else playing on **your mind.**

As a minimum, you need to record the task you were working on, the time, the reason for distraction, the cause and other findings if you wish to do so.

Below is an example of what a Distraction Log may look like. You can easily create one on a piece of paper or an electronic document. Don't make it too complicated, but include at least:

- Time of day
- Task you were working on
- The reason for losing focus
- The cause of distraction

Go for whatever works for you: pen and paper or electronic. The format doesn't matter as long as you record your logs accurately and honestly.

For instructions how to get a copy of a Distraction Log template I prepared for you, check the Bonuses section of this book.

DISTRACTION LOG					
Time	Place	Task	Reason for Distraction	Cause For Distraction	E/B/M?
6:30am	Office	Planning the report	Meowing cat	Hungry cat – forgot to feed her	E
7:15 am	Office	Same report, still planning stage	Can't concentrate, a bit dizzy	Hunger, haven't had breakfast yet	B
8:30am	Office	Writing the report	Phone ringing	Phone ringing	E
8:40	Office	Writing the report	Feeling angry	That b**y phone was ringing for 20 signals! I counted them!	M/E
9:45	Office	Formatting the report	Remembered that I should call Danny today	Trying to remember to call him	M
10:15	Office	Phone call to Danny	Another call on my landline	Ringing phone	M/E

Distraction Log Example

To get a good sense of your pattern(s), you should run those logs for a few days at least. Ideally, include one 'work cycle'—a period of time when you cover your most typical activities. For most people with most activities this will be a week (or a Monday—Friday period). But if you have several key activities you do in other than weekly intervals (e.g. bi-weekly meetings, or monthly assignments), you may consider running the logs for longer to include those activities.

IDENTIFYING PATTERNS

Once you've run Distraction Logs for at least a week, look at the data you've gathered. Are there **any patterns** there? Where do most of your distraction triggers come from? Is it your environment, your body or your mind? What's the most common distraction? What's the most common interruption?

To get to the bottom of the problem(s), you may need to do some detective work. The 'reason for losing focus'—the trigger, may differ from 'the cause of distraction'—the underlying problem. Don't get distracted by those triggers—dig deeper to find out what the underlying problem is.

When exploring the cause of your distraction, don't settle for the first thing that springs to your mind. The reason for your distraction will usually be the immediate trigger (e.g., the noise on the street outside your window), but the underlying cause may be different (e.g., the fact that your window was open, or that you were tired and more sensitive to noise than usually).

Go deeper, ask 'why,' and keep asking until you arrive at the core problem, or start circling around. You don't need to psychoanalyse everything, but the point of this exercise is to at least identify which of the three 'focus danger zones' the challenge is coming from: your environment, your body or your mind.

For example, if you are getting worried that you're running late, your anxiety is distracting you (so coming from your mind). But the reason for the worry is the fact that you're running late, and you're running late because you spent too much time trying to find stuff you needed for the job (environment). So the reason for distraction is your anxiety (mind), but the real cause of it is the fact that you have a messy desk (environment).

Or, if you're getting distracted by little noises in your environment that normally don't distract you (e.g. the sound of air-conditioning, or birds chirping outside your window), examine what else is going on with you. You may discover that you're unusually tired today (didn't sleep well last night), or hungry. So the reasons for your inability to focus will be in your environment (noise), but the cause is in your body (tired, hungry).

Always look at the situation from your own point of view, e.g., if you got distracted because of the argument next door, answers along the lines of 'because they've had a very loud argument' or 'the walls are too thin' are of little use to you. Instead, ask yourself HOW this specific situation has affected YOU. Why did you get distracted by the loud argument next door? Because you get anxious when people around you argue, or because you can't focus in a noisy environment, or (extreme example) they were arguing so loud the walls were shaking and so was your desk?

Framing the problem this way will enable you to see how you can influence your specific situation and change what's not working for you. You can't change the thickness of the walls or stop your neighbours from arguing (you can call the authorities if you feel this is appropriate, though), but you can do something about the noise in your office/study room.

As I mentioned before, it is likely there may be a couple of things pulling your attention away from your task at the same time. You need to take note of them all and try to track it back to the original trigger.

Now you know how to identify what's not working in your focus system, go ahead, grab a piece of (electronic) paper or your favourite app and track your distractions.

With at least a week's worth of data, you will be able to identify patterns in your struggles. Once you're clear on what needs fixing, have a look at the Laser-Sharp Focus Roadmap for further directions on where to find specific help.

In the next chapter I will tell you how setting clear goals can improve your focus.

	PROBLEM?	WHAT TO DO?	HOW TO DO IT?
A	I don't know what's wrong with my focus	Diagnose your situation	Run distraction logs/procrastination logs for a few days/a week **(Chapter 2)**
B	I feel overwhelmed, because I don't know what to do.	Clarify you goals	Identify your BIG Goal and break it down into smaller, sub-goals, make them SMART **(Chapter 3)**
C	I can't be bothered to work on this job/task/project	Review your motivation	Balance you intrinsic and extrinsic motivators **(Chapter 4)**
D	I feel uninspired /unmotivated /disinterested in this job/task/project	Boost your motivation	Review/refresh your motivation for doing the job-at-hand; use intrinsic and/or extrinsic motivators **(Chapter 4)**
E	I get distracted by noise/what's going on around me	Create a distraction-free environment	Eliminate/minimise noise and distractions, manage technology, find a quiet spot, use noise-cancelling earmuffs/ headphones **(Chapter 5)**

Table heading: WHAT'S YOUR BIGGEST PROBLEM?

F	I often check my phone/emails/ messages	As above	Turn off notifications, put phone on silent, close any unused applications **(Chapter 5)**
G	Other people distract/interrupt me	As above	Address the issue with people around you; find a quiet spot, use noise cancelling earmuffs/ headphones **(Chapter 5)**
H	I don't have enough energy to focus/complete my jobs, I often feel tired/run out of energy quickly	Discuss it with your doctor and address any underlying physical/mental health issues first. Are you sleeping and eating well? Taking breaks? Are you managing your energy?	Make sure you sleep enough, maintain good hydration and nutrition, schedule in breaks and rest **(Chapters 6 & 11)**
I	My back/eyes/neck hurts/is uncomfortable	Check with your doctor/healthcare provider and address any underlying health issues first. Is your workspace ergonomic?	Set up your desk, chair and overall workspace ergonomically, attend to any physical needs, sleep, nutrition, hydration, rest, exercise, breaks etc. **(Chapter 5 & 6)**

J	My mind often wanders off/ I daydream a lot	Are you managing your mind?	Learn how to prevent your mind from wandering off, and how to bring it back on track **(Chapter 7)**
K	I get distracted by my own thoughts	As above	Learn to bring your mind back on track **(Chapter 7)**
L	My negative thoughts get in the way	Check with your doctor and address any underlying mental health problems first. Learn to manage your negative thoughts	Recognise, acknowledge, let go/challenge your thoughts or ignore etc. **(Chapter 7)**
M	I struggle to concentrate when I'm emotional (happy/sad/upset/angry)	Check with your doctor and address any underlying mental health problems first. Are you able to manage your emotions?	Learn to use emotions to enhance your focus. Find the 'sweet spot' of emotional arousal. Manage stronger emotions **(Chapter 7)**
N	I procrastinate a lot	Find out why you procrastinate, use a strategy and use appropriate anti-procrastination tools.	Run procrastination log for a few days/ a week to understand your patterns. Use appropriate strategies (long term) or tactics (short term) **(Chapter 8)**

O	My attention span is too short	Talk to your doctor about any potential underlying physical and/or mental health issues. Learn how to extend your attention span	Address any issues with immediate attention in your environment, body and mind **(Chapters 5, 6, 7)** and gradually extend your attention span **(Chapter 11)**
P	I'm too stressed/anxious	Talk to your doctor and address any underlying physical and/or mental health issues. Learn how to harness stress to help you focus	Use stress management techniques to manage chronic stress; use acute stress (e.g. deadlines, accountability) to enhance your focus **(Chapter 12)**
Q	I forget to use my focus-enhancing strategies/I practice some focus strategies for a while and then fall off/forget	Develop a system to put your focus-enhancing strategies on autopilot	Use the habit loop (Cue/Behaviour/Reward) to create desired behaviours, create and use checklists, 'stack your habits' **(Chapter 13)**

Laser-Sharp Focus Roadmap Fig. 1

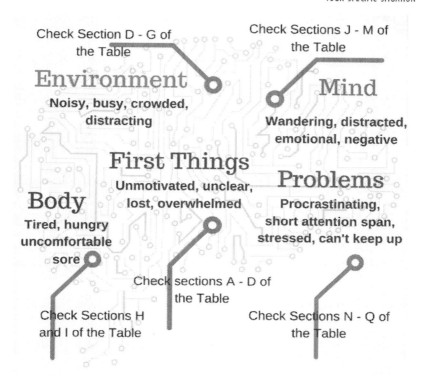

Laser-Sharp Focus Roadmap Fig. 2

For instructions how to get a pdf version of this table and a graphic representation of this map check the Bonuses section of this book.

CHAPTER 3 - SETTING GOALS: WHY IT'S IMPORTANT FOR BETTER FOCUS AND HOW TO DO IT

In this chapter I will zero in on an obvious, but very important aspect of creating a laser-sharp focus: goal setting. I will explain why goal setting is important for achieving greater clarity of focus, how to set long and short-term goals, and how to track your progress.

Goal setting—you've heard it all, haven't you? SMART goals, et al.

If you're already aware of why you need to set goals and how goal-setting is related to your productivity, effectiveness, and specifically focus, feel free to skip this chapter.

If you're not sure, not clear, or just need a refresher, keep reading. Below are a few evidence-based reasons.

WHY GOAL-SETTING IS IMPORTANT TO ACHIEVING BETTER FOCUS

Goal-setting is crucial to achieving what we want in life, and obviously what you want from your ability to focus.

Why?

Because the first step to succeeding in getting where you want to be is... knowing where you want to be.

If you don't know what you need/want to focus on, the best focusing skills in the world are not going to deliver tangible results.

Goal-setting helps distinguish relevant from irrelevant stuff. With clear vision, you are able to prioritise. As a result, you know what you should be working on right now and in the future.

Goal-setting is also a vital element of motivation. Clear goals will help you muster motivation for whatever your task at hand is. This is particularly important in situations when your long-term, intrinsic motivation gets a little lost behind the pile of day-to-day stuff to do.

People who set their own goals, make sure those goals are relevant to them and care about the outcomes are more committed to reach their goals. And obviously, the more committed to your goals you are, the better your performance and the bigger your chances of succeeding.

So get into a habit of setting goals for yourself. Read on to see how to do that.

How to set goals for a laser-sharp focus

1. Set your own meaningful goals

The goals you've set should be meaningful and relevant to you. If, for whatever reason, you are working towards goals set for you by others (e.g. your parents, teachers), or feel they are otherwise 'given'/forced on you, see if you can reframe them. When reframing 'goals given,' look for drivers you can relate to, stuff that is relevant and meaningful to you.

There is plenty of evidence that you are more likely to succeed if you are pursuing goals that are relevant and meaningful to you. Students who set their own educational goals perform much better academically than those who just 'plod along' or take what the teacher sets out for them. [1]

The same goes for employees—those who set their own personal standards for productivity achieve better results than those who have their goals set for them by the employer and are incentivised for their performance. [2]

This may sound obvious for people who grew up being encouraged to 'be their own person.' For those of you who are either not sure of yourself, or have some obligations towards your parents, spouses, children or family in general, this may be harder.

Many students asked me how they are supposed to 'set their own goals' when their goals have been set for them by their parents or society's expectations. I have also met parents—immigrants—who were pursuing goals set for their family's sake rather than their own professional or personal development.

Sometimes your situation influences your goals much more than your own wishes.

However, it does not mean that you're doomed. Like with the discovery of intrinsic factors under the cover of extrinsic motivation (we will discuss it in Chapter 4), I believe you can create your own goals that are meaningful to you within the constraints of what is given to you. The key is to understand what drives you and see how this is connected to the 'given goal.'

If, for whatever reason, you feel you are pursuing goals that are not completely yours, look beyond the surface. If you are following the wishes of your parents, you need to retrain because you have been made redundant, or you need to retake your exams because the country you have moved to does not recognise your qualification, explore what underpins that. You can either see 'what's in it for me,' use the 'given goal' as a means to an end, or just reframe it to include your own internal motivation.

For example, if your parents want you to become an accountant because they believe this would give you good job opportunities, financial security and social standing, and you would rather do something more risky but creative and fun, you could consider becoming an accountant as a means to an end. Your own meaningful goal could be that of quickly getting a job in a city to gain financial and emotional freedom to pursue your creative endeavours alongside the job, or at a later stage in life.

In the immigrant with unrecognised qualifications example, the external motivation is the ability to earn money to support your family. But the underlying, internal motivation may be that of wanting to practice your profession again, or to be able to get a job you're an expert in. It may also be a bigger-picture goal—to achieve financial freedom, or to give yourself or your family better quality of life, etc.

This exercise is similar to the one I suggest for exploring/refreshing your intrinsic motivation (Intrinsic Motivation Discovery Exercise) in the next chapter. Check it for more inspiration.

Remember, whatever it is you are pursuing, make sure you have a stake in the game and the goal is meaningful and relevant to you.

2. Set your goals as positive statements

Studies show that people are more likely to achieve goals framed positively than negative ones.

Reframe your goals if needed. Want to stop checking your FB and phone for new messages every few minutes to minimise disruption to your study time? Set yourself a goal of improving your productivity by managing technology.

Do you overcommit yourself for the fear of losing out and want to cut down on the number of projects you get involved in? Reframe your goal from 'I want to stop putting my hand up so often' to 'I want to be able to fully concentrate on 3 projects that are most relevant to me.'

3. Set ambitious goals

Multiple studies have shown that setting challenging goals leads to high levels of performance ([1,2,4]). Furthermore, challenging goals lead to a higher sense of self-efficacy—the perception of being able to do the task, which in turn further fuels motivation and the success cycle.

If you are familiar with the concept of **flow** (a.k.a. The Zone) described by Csikszentmihalyi [5], you may be aware that this fully immersed, energised state of focus happens when the right level of challenge meets the right level of skills. Challenges below your skill level are likely to lead to boredom and apathy, while tasks too difficult for your experience will create anxiety.

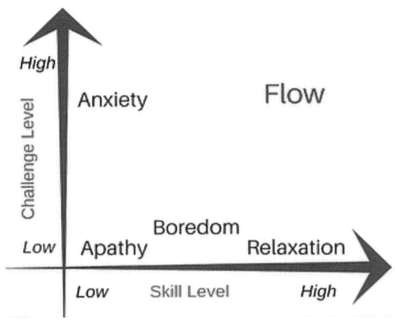

Model of Flow as a function of the level of skill vs the level of challenges as per Csikszentmihalyi [5]

4. Make your goals SMART

I'm sure we have all heard that old acronym, but let's go over it again.

SMART goals are Specific, Measurable, Attainable, Realistic, and Timely.

Why do they work better than broad, aspirational, 'do my best' kinds of goals?

For many reasons, including the initiation and on-going motivation effect of Implementation Intention ('if-then plan' goal achievement strategy, spelling out in advance how the person will go about achieving their goal), increase in self-efficacy, and the most obvious—the clarity of focus [6].

How do you make your goals SMART?

Here are a few suggestions:

SPECIFIC

Ask yourself the 5 W questions: who, what, where, when, why.

People who clearly describe how they're going to reach their goal are more likely to implement the plan they've come up with, e.g.:

Who: I

What: will complete the first draft of my novel by writing/will have market research completed

Where: in my office/talking face-to-face to my target audience 'in town'

When: every morning from 6 a.m. till 10 a.m./during lunch breaks

Why: because I want to have the manuscript ready for the competition so that I can get feedback on it/because I want to develop a thorough avatar for my start-up target audience (and so on).

MEASURABLE

Decide how you are going to measure your success. Is it by the number of in-person interviews completed (if you're an entrepreneur researching your market)? Progress in word count (if you're writing a novel)? Or maybe your grades (for students)?

Your measurements will depend on your goal. Be clear how you're going to track your progress and how you will know you have accomplished your goal.

ATTAINABLE

Ask yourself an honest question: Do you really have all it takes to get there? Do you have any skill, knowledge, or equipment gaps? And if you do lack something, can you acquire, develop, or somehow make up for those gaps?

REALISTIC

A common reason many goals end up not being achieved is underestimating how much time and effort 'getting there' requires.

Be realistic in setting up the 'by when' and estimating the financial and effort implications of pursuing your goal.

Fledgling entrepreneurs and wannabes juggling regular jobs and their new businesses often underestimate the energy toll this approach takes. If you are embarking on a journey where such 'burning the candle at both ends' is involved, consider managing your energy rather than your time. Check *Chapter 11: The Importance of Managing Energy, Not Time* for tips on how to manage your energy.

TIMELY

For best results, have a deadline for your efforts. Deadlines are great for pushing on, particularly when you need that extra motivation to finish.

Some people really thrive under time pressure, and often leave their tasks to the last moment—then with that deadline closely hanging over their heads, they are able to muster extra energy and get to the finish line. The upsides are clear: with adrenaline-fueled buzz and excitement, the job gets done in a tick. But the trade-offs are common and potentially harmful: unnecessary stress, higher potential for things to go wrong and hence delays due to no time buffer.

However, if you prefer a more planned, consistent and systematic approach to your work, set out whatever timeline may suit you best. Do whatever fits your working style and your needs. The point here is to ground your goal within a time frame.

> ** Note: these rules apply to performance and ability goals—that is, goals revolving around tasks, projects or skill-learning, but are not quite applicable to habit-formation or habit changing. **

Use these steps when setting up your educational, performance, or production goals, such as:

- I want to learn how to build iOS apps over the next few months
- I want to run a half marathon by the end of this year
- I want to release my book on July 1st

but not for things such as establishing habits and behaviours, e.g.,

- I want to practice meditation every morning
- I want to develop a regular exercise/study routine
- I want to meaningfully participate in team meetings

5. Start with the Big Goal and work from there

This strategy for planning your journey will help you keep your motivation well-fuelled (see Chapter 4 for more details) in the longer and shorter run. It also helps with prioritising your tasks.

WHEN YOU FIRST SET YOUR GOALS, START WITH THE BIG PICTURE IN MIND

How to do it?

On a large piece of paper, or electronic document, or in any mind-mapping software:

- If you're using paper/white board, at the top of the page write down your Big Goal: the who, what, where, when and why of your goal. Remember to be SMART.
- At the bottom of the page write where you are now
- Map the major steps necessary to get from where you are to where you want to be
- Work out what your sub-goals and milestones are to make sure you capture all the steps necessary.
- Add timelines/deadlines

You can also use mind mapping or other non-linear tools, using hardware (pen & paper, pen/whiteboard) or software. Mind maps are good for keeping track of all sub-goals and side threads. I prefer using pen & paper, but software has the benefit of easily collapsing multiple branches and sub-threads for clarity.

Spend as much time as you need on this exercise. Come back to your plan/map and update it regularly. You may want to review the goals after some time. The document will grow and evolve, and that's okay.

The key is to keep the map/plan relevant to what you want in life and capture what really matters to you.

Let's say you want to quit your day job and start a health & fitness business. Your main driver is your passion for health and fitness, and the dream of working for yourself and financial independence.

Having a successful health & fitness business is your Big Goal.

The major steps (sub-goals) may include:

- Completing a qualification in health & fitness
- Saving up some money
- Creating a business plan for your new business
- Setting up the business
- Creating your first program to offer to your clients
- Making your first money by selling your program
- Quitting your job
- Scaling up the business

Anything you do should be connected with your Big Picture Goal(s). If you constantly catch yourself working on something that is not included in your plan, not connected to your goals, you should be asking yourself if the plan needs updating (to include the goals stemming from those tasks), or whether you are using your time appropriately.

My friend and productivity guru, Tor Refsland, developed a system that helps connect your Big Picture Goal(s) with your everyday goals. He calls it the DUMB SMART goal system. The idea is to connect your Inspirational (Dreaming Uplifting Massive Cojones* and Barely Attainable—DUMB) goal with the classically written SMART goals that form the stepping stones to your Inspirational goal. He has used this system to achieve many goals in his professional and personal life. He has also helped other people achieve their goals through this simple, but powerful system—see below.

(*Cojones means balls in Spanish)

Take your Dreaming Uplifting Massive cojones and Barely attainable goal and break it down into smaller manageable goals (make them SMART) Example: Your DUMB goal is to earn $12,000 more per year.

You break the yearly goal down into 12 months, which means that you need to make $1,000 per month in order to hit your goal. (This can again be broken down into smaller goals, like weeks and days.)

Then you identify the key income-generating activities that will bring you closer to earning those $1, 000 per month, which turns out to be activity A, B, C, D and E. (Make sure they are Specific, Measurable... etc.)

Then you focus on ONLY doing those activities. That will bring you closer to your goal.

If you want to become very productive so you crush your goals fast, you need master the ability of focus.

The ability to enter *the zone *at will*,* where you become extremely productive in a certain period of time, can only be achieved by becoming laser-focused.

In order to do that it`s essential that you:

1. Remove all distractions

2. Know what specific task you are going to do

3. Focus on working on the single task at hand until it`s finished (if you have a big task, break it down into smaller tasks.)"

It may seem daunting in the start, but start small in the beginning. You can do it!

Find out more about Tor's goal-achieving system on his website and grab a copy of his free book and exclusive course on turbocharging your productivity: http://www.timemanagementchef.com/joanna

According to Scott Dinsmore of Live Your Legend [7], Warren Buffett, one of the wealthiest people in the world, recommends a 2-list approach to goal setting. Once you've narrowed down your goals to top-25, create two lists:

List A: with your top-5 goals, to which you commit yourself fully

List B: with the remaining 20—these become your 'avoid-at-all-cost' anti-goals.

Why? You have a limited amount of time and energy available. If you really want to achieve your goals, make sure you spend your time and energy on things that truly matter to you. Everything else becomes waste and hence should be avoided at all cost.

If you're **already underway with your goals**, every time you're considering getting involved into a new project, or activity—check how it fits with your Big Goal(s) map/plan. And if it does, make sure you understand the connections. If it's not connected, it's likely to be not aligned with your current goals. Ask yourself an honest question: do I really want to spend my time and energy doing this?

Dump, delegate, or defer.

LONG-TERM GOALS VS. SHORT-TERM GOALS

To be honest, scientists are not all that clear on the outcomes from short-term and long-term goals. Some studies showed that short-term goals are more likely to be achieved, but others have proven it's the other way round.

At the end of the day, it really is about what works for you.

As I said above, it's important to always keep in mind your Big Goals, which are usually long-term in nature. It improves your motivation and commitment to them.

But, if you are a short-distance runner, like me, and you struggle to keep on track if you can't see the finish line, you will have problems training for a marathon, literally and metaphorically.

With bigger long-term goals I make sure to map out milestones, breaking them down into smaller steps and have some early 'wins'/quick goals, too. This way, I can focus on what's immediately in front of me/just round the corner, knowing that I am working towards my long-term goal rather than just chasing the next shiny object.

TRACKING YOUR PROGRESS

Once you've got your map/plan and your measure of success (see p. 3), set up a tracking system.

Why?

Because even the best goals in the world are useless if we don't keep on track with them.

The simplest way of keeping an eye on your progress is keeping your goals visible and reviewing them regularly.

There are many ways in which you can keep your goals visible:

- Put them up on the wall
- Have your Map/Plan pinned up on the board
- Write down in your diary/calendar, etc.
- With your map/plan in front of you, schedule reviews and book them in your calendar.
- Choose intervals that align with your milestones and key sub-goals so that you have enough time to achieve what you've set yourself up, e.g., if you are working towards your health & fitness qualification (as in the example above), you may want to schedule quick check-ins on your progress every term. If you are writing a book and set yourself a daily or weekly writing goal, check in at those time marks.
- For longer term goals or more fluid ones, such as developing a skill/ability or saving money, you can check your progress in fixed intervals, such as monthly, quarterly, yearly etc.
- Always check your progress against the planned goals using the measurement you've decided on.

People often ask me what tools they should use for tracking progress. My answer is: use whatever works for you. If you are a pen & paper person, like me—use it. If you prefer technology solutions—find something that may work for you.

There are many apps and other software tools to help keep track of progress. They change so often (some disappear, while new apps appear), it's hard to recommend anything. Use your favourite browser to find out what's trending. Remember rule number 1: it has to be something easy to use and fit into your life. The best progress-tracking software is only as good as your manual inputs.

Many people find that 'ticking things off' from their to-do lists give them satisfaction, a sense of fulfilment. If this is your case, go for it. Put a tick in your diary or beside the milestone on your Map/Plan, cross it off on your calendar. You can even create a timeline with your goals/deadlines on it and tick/cross them all off as you progress towards your finishing line.

Goal setting is a very broad topic and there is lots of information on how to do it available out there. I'm aware I've just touched the tip of the iceberg in this chapter, but hopefully I've managed to show you how good goal-setting can improve your focus. I also walked you through the steps to effective goal-setting and monitoring the progress.

In the next chapter, we will look at motivation and its role in focus and concentration. I will express my views on the evergreen issue of the need to 'motivate yourself.' I may have some shocking surprises for you

.

CHAPTER 4 - MOTIVATION: TO MOTIVATE OR NOT TO MOTIVATE AND WHY I BELIEVE 'GETTING MOTIVATED' IS OVERRATED

How do I motivate myself to focus? Have you ever asked yourself or anyone else this question?

Have you put any inspirational quotes up in your study/office or on your screensaver?

Do you wish you could find a way to 'keep motivated' to stay focused on your task until it's finished?

You're not alone.

You also may be wrong.

In this chapter we will consider:

- Why motivation does not really matter in developing good focus habits
- How to spot when poor motivation is affecting your focus
- The most common motivation problems and how to deal with them

I will also show you how to discover your own long-lasting intrinsic motivation, and how to find motivation to complete that dreaded job-at-hand.

Here is my little motivation secret: more often than not, your motivation is not a problem.

How come?

Since you've got this book and you've read it until this page, I'm sure you're not only aware you have a problem with your ability to focus, you also likely to have an idea what the nature of your problem is. You may have tried to fix it before and have made some progress. But you have not given up—you are still keen to get it sorted.

All that means you are really motivated to be able to focus and remained focused.

See?

Your motivation may not be strong, or may be of a kind you're not happy about, but as long as you try to address your focus problem, it is there.

Call me cynical if you want, but I gave up on 'inspirational-motivational fluff' long time ago. Why?

Because, even though it's very important to achieving your goals in life, motivation is too unreliable.

> *"We all have goals. And what's the first thing most of us think about when we consider how to achieve them?*
>
> *'I need to get motivated.'*
>
> *The surprising thing? Motivation is exactly what you don't need.*
>
> *Motivation is short-lived and doesn't lead to consistent action. If you want to achieve your goals, then you need a plan for exactly _when_ and _how_ you're going to execute them."*
>
> James Clear, Achieve Your Goals [1]

Motivation is a matter of feelings. "Do you feel motivated to read this book?" I may ask you. And if you say "Yes, of course," that's great. But if you are not—well, what can you do? You may want to wait to feel motivated again or look for ways to 'get motivated.'

The feeling of being motivated is just like any other feeling. It is multifactorial and complex, and hence, difficult to sustain and rely on in our day-to-day mundane life.

Motivation comes and goes.

Yes, we are driven by motivation. Whether it's wanting to help others, look pretty or just minimise your efforts (a.k.a. be lazy) you will be aiming at doing what you feel motivated to achieve.

Moreover, it's very hard to work against your motivation. A friend of mine had a dream of helping people by making them feel happier, and happier about themselves. Her parents and bigger family believed she would be an excellent doctor, so they insisted she attend medical school. So she duly did. But she was very unhappy there. She was really struggling to make herself study for long hours, or listen during lectures. She was failing exams. She was becoming sick more and more often. Yes, she felt she was studying to help others, but not quite in a way that was aligned with who she was. She valued beauty and was quite interested in how our own mind and self-beliefs affect how we perceive beauty. When she dropped out of med school, she became a beautician. She felt happier helping women feel good about themselves, but still she believed there was a gap. Eventually, she went back to college to pursue qualifications in counselling. She is a very fulfilled and very successful counsellor specialising in helping women discover their inner beauty and shine.

Working against your motivation is not only hard—it can be heart-wrenching and soul-destroying.

But often people become too attached to motivation and getting motivated. Let me say it again, it's great to feel motivated because it makes the journey toward your goals a lot easier, but it is natural that motivation fluctuates. Motivation can change depending on your mood, your sleep, your meals, physical health, hormones, stress, circumstances. Have you ever experienced a drop (or an increase) in motivation following a small setback?

What about just plain passage of time? Do you still remember your New Year Resolution? How did you do on that?

Only about 46% of people who made New Year resolutions actually keep them after 6 months. Worse, 30% drop it after 2 weeks. Here is how unreliable motivation can be. [2]

As I mentioned above, since you are reading this book, I'm assuming you have motivation to improve your focus. However, it may be that your motivation is not strong enough, or of the 'wrong kind.'

How to spot poor motivation affecting your focus

As I said before, difficulty in focusing may be caused by many things, and poor motivation for the task/job at hand is one of them.

How do you know it is your poor motivation that is affecting your ability to focus?

Poor motivation or lack of motivation typically manifests itself by **lack of energy and enthusiasm** for the task you are supposed to focus on. You may be dragging your feet to start on the job, thinking 'I can't be bothered to do that,' 'I don't like it' (or even: 'I hate it!'), 'What's the point of [doing] this,' or, 'This is stupid/boring/useless!' Or you may be even doing the actual job, while still muttering those things under your breath or out loud.

The key is, for whatever reason, you don't feel motivated to focus on whatever you should be doing, despite all the potential or real consequences of not doing so.

On the surface, you may procrastinate and get easily distracted by all sorts of more interesting things. Be mindful that procrastination and the tendency to get easily distracted can be frequently driven by other issues. Often people assume that procrastination equals lack of motivation for the job at hand, but this may not be the case. Procrastination can indicate a wide range of underlying issues (see Chapter 8 for more details) so do not assume your procrastination or distraction problem is in fact a motivation problem.

Here are a few questions to help you decide if you have a motivation problem:

- Why am I doing this instead of what I **should** be doing?

- How does the task I should be working on make me feel? Lazy? Flat? Bored? Uninspired? Unmotivated? 'Can't be bothered/whatever?'

If your answer aligns with what's described above, you are likely to have a motivation problem.

Remember that motivation fluctuates. Even though you may not feel it right now, at some point you were interested in the job or the subject. You probably saw value in it, even if you did not like it, or found it too much of a burden.

Explore your motivation for agreeing to do the job/task, or study the subject/topic in the first instance.

What is it? Write it down.

Let's now look at how motivation works and some common motivation problems and how to fix them.

How motivation works

From the psychological point of view, motivation can either come from within the person (**intrinsic motivation**), or be driven by external factors (**extrinsic motivation**).

Extrinsic motivation can work quite well, but its appeal usually wears off after some time, or when you run out of rewards to collect.

Intrinsic motivation is much more powerful and lasting. It fuels people to pursue their goals over a number of years, if not their entire lifespans. It is driven by passion, internal fire and the deepest human desires to achieve mastery, personal fulfilment and autonomy. These are all big words, yes, so the downside of intrinsic motivation is that it sometimes fails us in day-to-day, dull-as-hell situations.

In order for your motivation to work well for you in the short and long run, you need a powerful, long-lasting intrinsic motivator to guide you and some short-term extrinsic strategies you can use for the day-to-day struggles.

THE MOST COMMON MOTIVATION PROBLEM

The more I learn about it, the more I believe that the most common motivation problem is the wrong mixture of intrinsic and extrinsic motivators.

SCENARIO 1: YOUR DOMINANT (OR ONLY) MOTIVATION IS EXTRINSIC IN NATURE

How do you tell you are (mainly) driven by extrinsic motivation?

As said above, extrinsic motivation relies on rewards, compensation, avoiding punishment, doing things for other people's sake, to get their approval or praise, e.g.,

You're doing a job/tasks/project because:

- It brings money or some other material reward (e.g., bonus payment/reward, new tools) even as small as a bar of chocolate
- You'll get an immaterial reward (trip to the beach, 30 minutes of your favourite game, 'employee of the month' badge, promotion/good grades)
- To keep an important person/people (parents, boss, teachers, etc.) happy, gain their approval, avoid disapproval or anger
- To get noticed by an influential person
- You want to keep up a certain image of yourself (e.g., as someone successful, helpful, caring) or to 'keep up with the Joneses'
- To avoid punishment (e.g., paying fines, being ridiculed, ostracised, rejected)

These are all examples of extrinsic drivers to your actions. If you often struggle to focus because of low motivation, chances are it's because your motivation is not strong enough, which usually is a sign of extrinsic motivation being the main driver.

So what's the problem?

Reward-driven motivators can work, but they often turn out to be short-lived and their impact wears out quickly. If your main motivation for the task at hand is extrinsic, you are likely to experience a drop in motivation as the time goes on or the task requires more effort. So a bar of chocolate can take you through a boring chapter or two, but may not be enough to motivate you to prepare for a large exam. The thought of becoming an employee of the month and getting a raise may give you a boost needed to complete that boring project, but you will quickly forget about it and struggle to motivate yourself again soon.

What you can do to improve it

Refresh/Rediscover your intrinsic drivers

If you are struggling to focus because you are lacking motivation, review your motivation for doing the task at hand. It may be that you have an intrinsic motivation to pursue the overall goals, but you may have forgotten about it or 'can't see the wood for the trees.'

When I was at the university, I struggled a lot with this type of scenario. Often, my life was punctuated with exams, and all I could see was one thing to tick off after another. And while getting those exams and subjects 'ticked off' was bringing a sense of achievement, I had to regularly remind myself of my overall goal—becoming a doctor and helping others—to boost my motivation and push through.

If you find yourself being driven by external rewards, don't despair. In my experience, extrinsic motivators are often not as superficial as they seem. If you explore your reasons for pursuing what you are pursuing right now in more depth, you may find more intrinsic motives underneath.

I believe that even extrinsic motivators, such as financial rewards, praise or privileges, can be turned into or reframed as intrinsic motivators. We will look at intrinsic motivators in more depth in a minute, but to give you an idea:

Rewards, particularly financial, are usually about achieving financial independence, or being able to afford pursuit of hobbies or passions.

Similarly, seeking praise may be really about feeling that your job is valued by others, and further, feeling that you are contributing to the community.

From this perspective, your evening coding job to earn some money may actually be a way of achieving financial independence, and hence autonomy. The marketing campaign you've volunteered for to get noticed and promoted is really about seeking mastery in the art of marketing.

Look beyond the surface and the extrinsic reasons why, explore your own deeper motives. Don't feel embarrassed. This is not just an exercise in 'information management'—reframing your motivation really works and can have a powerful effect on your ability to push on with your work or your studies, and focus better.

To find your intrinsic motivation, seek how your current goals are connected with your deeper desires of mastering a skill or knowledge, of becoming autonomous or pursuing a noble goal, your personal mission.

Discover your intrinsic motivation

Okay, you may say, but what if I don't have any intrinsic motivation? Am I doomed?

No, you're not.

If you haven't discovered your intrinsic motivation yet, or you have forgotten about it, you may want to embark on the Intrinsic Motivation Discovery Exercise:

Intrinsic Motivation Discovery Exercise

This is a really simple exercise created more to refine or clarify your intrinsic motivation than to find a life purpose. If you feel you need to discover what your passion or personal mission is, you may need to put some time aside to do discover how to do that.

EXERCISE:

Grab a piece of paper (or create an electronic document).

1. Ask yourself WHY you're doing what you're doing, e.g., Ed is working on an assignment as part of an app development course. Why? Because he wants to complete the course.

2. Write down your answer and check it against the Three Main Intrinsic Motivators.

Can your reason(s) for doing this [thing] be described as working to achieve autonomy, mastery (or a subject, skill, area) or by pursuing a passion/noble goal? If yes, then you've got it.

3. If not—go back to your answer and ask yourself: WHY?

Once you've got the answer—again check it against Autonomy/Mastery/Purpose trio.

Repeat until you can clearly assign your motivation to one or more categories. Let's look at Ed's example now

Why does Ed want to complete the app development course?
- Because he wants to develop his own app.

Why?
- Because he wants to start his own business and make money.

Why?
- Because he wants to earn enough money to travel and explore the world. (This answer already hints at pursuit of Autonomy, but we can explore even further.)

Why?
- Because he enjoys learning about other cultures and wants to be able to do that whenever he likes (Mastery and Autonomy).

4. Write it down and keep it handy.

Once you're clear on your Intrinsic Motivator, write it down and keep it handy. Go back and revisit regularly, particularly at times of struggle, when you feel this is all pointless and you'd rather be doing something else. If your motivation is truly about bigger goals, a sense of purpose, it will last.

RECORD IT FOR FUTURE USE

Once you have reviewed your motivation—whether just to refresh your memory and remind yourself you have an intrinsic motivation for doing what you do, or to reframe your extrinsic drivers into more internally driven ones, write it down. I suggest you write it several times in various places, just like you would do with your personal mission statement—your diary, your fridge, the welcome screen of your laptop—places where you're likely to see it often. Or, if you don't feel comfortable with this approach, put it somewhere where only you can see it, but look at it often, remind yourself about what is really driving you to pursue your goals.

SCENARIO 2: YOUR DOMINANT (OR ONLY) MOTIVATION IS INTRINSIC IN NATURE

HOW TO TELL YOU ARE (MAINLY) DRIVEN BY INTRINSIC MOTIVATION?

Intrinsic motivation comes from within you and is powered by your own dreams, aspirations, wants and wishes. It usually can be boiled down to the three following desires:

- Mastery
- Autonomy, or
- Purpose [3]

Motivation that relies on one or more of those three drivers tends to last longer and be more powerful. Typically, this is a type of motivation that gives people strength to pursue their dreams and aspirations, to fulfil their missions throughout their lives.

Let's look at it more closely now.

MASTERY

The road to mastery is a great aspiration, particularly for those pursuing education or professional expertise. It also works great for hobbies. Overall, anything which is skill or knowledge-based, from learning another language, to learning to cook, to becoming the master coder, or being able to fix a car, can be an example of mastery-driven motivation.

AUTONOMY

The desire to be autonomous is another great intrinsic motivator. Many successful people, particularly solopreneurs, are driven by financial or location independence, freedom to do what they love doing, or a desire to have a lifestyle they enjoy.

PURPOSE

For many people, motivation comes from a desire to pursue or fulfil a personal mission. Passion, purpose, noble goals, however this is called, it is about having an aspirational goal, usually open-ended and not necessarily achievable within the person's lifetime. This does not have to be 'larger than life' goal, but usually it is not only about you, but others and helping others.

Health professionals, teachers and counsellors are often driven by this kind of intrinsic motivators. But the desire to help others can be more practical too, with personal missions such as building safe homes, or even like my old friend from med school—helping people discover their inner beauty.

Many people combine more than just one driver. Often, you see a combination of pursuing the mastery of a skill in order to serve others, or achieving autonomy to pursue their mission in life. You can have all three present as well. The more, the better.

Typically, a person driven intrinsically feels they do things because they

- Want to become financially/emotionally/legally independent
- Want to pursue a certain lifestyle
- Want to help others achieve their goals
- Enjoy working with people/animals/plants/books/ideas/computers

- Love learning new stuff or are interested in a certain subject/topic
- Want to be the best in the bunch/world/country at this particular thing
- Enjoy sharing, contributing, being part of, belonging

SO WHAT'S THE PROBLEM?

Intrinsic motivation is great; it's the king of motivations, if I may say so. It is what makes people work for hours without even noticing they're working. It's fantastic to be powered by it, but sometimes it may be not enough.

In the day-to-day struggles, we can forget about those noble goals. Often, little mundane jobs that need to be done on time limit our point of view.

The physical challenges of ENT (Ear, Nose, and Throat) examination during my rotation and the brutal reality of what's inside the human ear or nose left a serious dent on my intrinsic motivation to become a doctor. I was only a few months away from finishing medical school and seriously considering quitting. It took me a lot of little, extrinsic rewards (chocolate, collaborating with my study buddy, competing for better grades) and willpower to get through that rotation. For me, it is a good example of a situation where extrinsic drivers can boost intrinsic motivation.

WHAT YOU CAN DO TO IMPROVE IT

You don't have to rely on chocolate or moping to your friends. With a carefully crafted approach, you can add little extrinsic boosters to your intrinsic motivation.

You can do it in two ways: by boosting your intrinsic motivation, or by applying some short-term extrinsic strategies. Pick and choose your preferred approach, or mix and match.

REFRESH YOUR INTRINSIC MOTIVATION

If you still remember what your intrinsic motivation for the job at hand is, a quick refresher is usually enough. Say it out loud, write it down and put it up on the wall, keep it in your secret drawer. Whatever works for you.

I do recommend writing it down and keeping the note handy so you can just look at it in times of doubt and motivational drain.

Deploy a quick extrinsic fix

There is nothing wrong with an external motivator now and then, when needed, as long as you don't abuse it and as long as it helps you get the job done.

What I tend to do depends on the situation at hand. Usually a quick reminder of the bigger purpose behind the dreaded task and a little 'extrinsic trick' do the job.

How to find an extrinsic motivator to complete that dreaded job-at-hand

Many of us have our own favourite extrinsic motivators, be it a bar of chocolate, a few minutes of your fav game, or some other material reward. But if you're lacking in inspiration, here are a few ideas:

- Is this task connected to some reward system, be it material or non-material rewards (e.g., rankings, grades, bonus points)? Can you use it to push yourself to get it done?
- Can you offer yourself a material or non-material reward for completing the task? Think your favourite treat, a (period of time) doing your favourite activity, 'letting yourself off the hook' with a (non-essential) chore
- Can you use it to 'boast' or get approval/praise from anyone/someone important (c'mon, it may not be the nicest or most mature thing to do, but if it works for you and doesn't harm anyone—why not?)
- Will you, by completing this task, avoid some sort of punishment, such as late payment penalty, bad grade, being criticised?

These are just a few examples. Never do anything that may hurt or harm other people, or yourself. Be careful not to overdo it and don't use it too often. Too much extrinsic motivation can kill your intrinsic motivation and you may end up not doing much at all. This phenomenon is called motivation crowding or the over-justification effect.

Behavioural economists and gamification experts are particularly aware of it, knowing that external rewards, such as money, fines, or points and badges would only affect the behaviour to a certain degree. And even if the person is internally motivated to continue with the behaviour, the fact that he/she is being motivated by external rewards may reduce the likelihood of him/her continuing with it. I have read about people who loved what they did so much they did it for free, but lost the drive to do it once they started being paid for the same job. Somehow, once what used to be 'fun' became a 'proper job,' the intrinsic motivation went down.

Developing or boosting your intrinsic drivers is a great way of dealing with poor motivation and hence improving your focus. It is handy to always have a few extrinsic tricks up your sleeve in case your big goal is not quite doing the job of motivating you at the time.

However, as I said at the very beginning of this chapter, motivation is by nature fluctuating and hence cannot be relied on. It is much better to build a reliable, repeatable system that would propel you into that laser-sharp focus every time you want and need it.

In the next chapter, I will show you how you can build an environment that helps you focus, whatever your motivation.

PART 2 -

SET UP YOUR

'FOCUS SYSTEM'

CHAPTER 5 -
BUILD AN ENVIRONMENT
THAT FACILITATES YOUR FOCUS

The second part of this book is dedicated to creating a robust system that will help you set your focus on an autopilot. I will cover three main aspect of a successful focus system: an environment that facilities your focus, a body optimised for maximum cognitive powers, and a well-managed mind.

In the first chapter, I show you how to set up an environment that is distraction-free and enhances your ability to focus so that you can get your jobs done faster, better and even enjoy it. Specifically, I will discuss:

- Why the right environment matters (and matters more than motivation)
- How to build a focus-enhancing workspace even if you don't have an office
- Making your workspace ergonomic, even on a tight budget
- Minimising noise
- Taking control of technology before it takes control of you

Oh, it's gone again....

Just as you felt you were going to get that job done, your phone beeped, a message flashed on your screen, or you had to get up to find a missing file. And now, your focus is gone. You're distracted, frustrated, with your heart pounding and your eyes skimming the environment for a clue as what you were supposed to do.

You feel like screaming. How on earth are you supposed to get back to your job now?

Does it feel familiar?

You really want to get your job done on time, to the best of your abilities, within budget. You want to work better, faster, more effectively, because your professional success, work-life balance, and even happiness depends on it.

You need to be able to get stuff done quickly, without errors, and with all your mental capacity switched on.

In a nutshell—with your mental focus FULL ON.

I totally get it.

But where is the blimmin' 'ON' button?

Well...

A few of years ago during my MBA studies, I came across the concept of behavioural economics and things such as choice architecture and nudging. The idea that decision processes and environment can make us change behaviour sounded hard to believe at first. But the evidence was overwhelming. Constructing narrow choice options in the way that gently nudge you toward 'the right one' works.

The most famous example is the percentage of people who agree to become organ donors. In the countries where you have to opt in to become a donor ('if you want to become an organ donor, tick here') far fewer people agree to donate their organs, compared with the countries with 'presumed consent('if you don't want to become an organ donor, tick here').' [1] To be fair, this difference may not be just the result of the way the system is designed, but it definitely plays a role.

The choice is still yours—you can opt out if you don't want to, but the way the environment of this decision-making process is set up can make an incredible difference.

Okay, but what does it have to do with focus?

WHY THE RIGHT ENVIRONMENT MATTERS (AND MATTERS MORE THAN MOTIVATION)

I used to struggle with a short attention span (and before you ask, no, I definitely do not have ADHD or ADD, I'm just a victim of the plain 'multitasking plague'). I used to spend hours 'on research,' but in fact just chasing shiny objects and fighting boredom by jumping from one task to another, getting up to make myself a cup of tea, go to the bathroom, do this or that. It got to the point where I could only maintain my focus for a couple of minutes and was constantly staying up late to not to miss deadlines.

One day, after I nearly missed a very important deadline, I decided enough was enough—no more rushes to the finish line, no more sleepless nights, no more opportunities lost to distractions and multitasking. I would chain myself to my desk if that was what I needed, I decided.

I did not chain myself to the desk literally, but keeping myself physically at my desk was one of the first steps to success. With each and every step, my productivity soared: I was getting stuff done much faster, with better quality. I was able to focus instantaneously and developed an ability to work in busy airport lounges and even on the plane.

To my surprise, my creativity did not die either. On the contrary—I got into a habit of sitting down to just write the next chapter without waiting for the ever-elusive 'inspiration.' I wrote a novel during a NaNoWriMo (National Novel Writing Month) twice, one of them while working full time, studying for my MBA and having a family and a life as well.

And as I worked on refining my system and did more research, I discovered that the most productive people, those who need to just sit down and turn their computer on to instantly become focused, shared a few commonalities. The more research I did, the clearer it become—the secret to instant focus that lasts until you're ready to finish your job for the day is... the right environment.

So stop blaming yourself and cursing your willpower, and dump that quest for motivation. You're not lazy or stupid—you've been misguided. Most people think that when it comes to focusing on work, study, a book, whatever it is you should be doing, the key is motivation. But you already know motivation is based on emotions, the way we feel in the moment, and hence, by nature ever-changing, unreliable and elusive. Join the uber-productive crew—redesign your environment.

If you have done your Distraction Logs, as I suggest in Chapter 2, you will have an idea where your specific focus difficulties are. I am assuming, since you are reading this chapter, that your environment is likely to be a potent source of all sorts of anti-focus traps.

Let's fix them one by one now.

CREATE A 'BRAIN-POWERS BOOSTING' WORKSPACE EVEN IF YOU DON'T HAVE AN OFFICE

Where do you usually work or study? Do you have your own study or workspace? Is it a desk or a table? Do you have your own study room/office? Or do you share it with anyone? And if you are a student, do you use communal study areas, like libraries or student quiet rooms?

Whatever it is, you need to make sure your workspace is geared to support your ability to concentrate on the job at hand.

If you tend to work/study while lying in bed, or sitting on a sofa, or somewhere else, consider shifting to a proper work or study space, preferably a desk, or a table and a comfortable chair. Beds are for sleeping, sofas are for relaxing and slouching—if you have been trying to learn/work in bed or on the sofa and wondering why you can't focus properly—here is your answer.

Your study area or workstation, and your desk in particular, are critical to your overall performance. You'll know what I'm talking about if you ever tried working on a coffee table or really hard chair with your computer screen too high and a window behind you flooding your monitor with glare.

"Okay, okay," I can hear you say, "But I learn best when I'm sitting comfortably on the sofa," "I've been working in the library/garden/cafés and it's fine," or "I don't have a dedicated study/office, I need to manage with what I've got."

Fair enough, not everyone can afford to have a specific room dedicated to intellectual work. And of course, it's always down to whatever works for you individually. But work space does not have to be big or fancy—it can be as simple as a dining table, which you can use at specific times. Or an old school desk in a corner of your shed/garage. And for those who use public space: libraries, study/quiet rooms, or even cafés and public gardens—I'd urge you to try and use those tips, too. Or you may want to try to set up a study/workspace in your own home.

For all of you, sceptical of what I'm suggesting: you can always run an experiment, measuring your ability to focus as expressed by your productivity (time spent on your task/job until completion or other outcome) when working in your usual space and by working in an environment set up as I suggest below.

How to build a focus-enhancing workspace, even if you don't have an office

If you have an office or a study room, you may have the problem solved. Or not—as it is in my case. Even though we do have an office in our house, I don't like that space: it's freezing cold on dull days, always cluttered, and it's full of my husband's stuff. I only use the office when I have something to record or a piece of work that needs doing during the weekend. I much prefer the dining table. I have my own little cabinet where I keep my work stuff so that I can quickly get it out and then put away when needed.

So what's a good working space?

Some of you may like it warmer or cooler, brighter or duller, with the window facing the garden or a blank garage wall. There are factors that depend on your preferences, but this is what the most productive people recommend:

- **Quiet space**—it does not have to be in complete silence, but the level of noise should not disturb you. Typical culprits include: street noise, animals or people, household appliances, TV/Radio/other sources of music and other noise.
- As **distraction-free** as possible (this is quite individual and I'd recommend you test if it works for you or not)
- Where **other people can't disturb you;** the point here is to limit/eliminate any opportunity for others approaching you 'just to ask

you a question, since you're sitting here...' or wanting to chat, or even saying 'hello' when passing by.

- This is particularly difficult if you're working in a shared office, an open plan office, or a communal/family area. Ideally, try to find a space where you would not be disturbed. If you can't, check Chapter 9 for tips on dealing with distraction in your environment.

Some productivity fanatics like their work space/offices to be completely deprived of anything that can potentially distract them: pictures, family photographs, view from the window. I've heard/read of people working while facing an empty, white wall.

This may be too extreme for you, but look around your workspace and check if there is anything in the environment that has ever distracted you. Maybe it's that wobbling table leg, or a squeaky chair. Or maybe that holiday photograph on your desk. Observe and eliminate or minimise if possible.

MAKING YOUR WORKSPACE ERGONOMIC, EVEN ON A TIGHT BUDGET

Ergonomics is a discipline concerned with human factors, interactions with environment, and optimisation of human well-being and overall system performance. The physical domain of ergonomics focuses on the human body at work: posture, handling of material, workplace layout, lighting, etc.

> "The benefits of an ergonomically correct work space have long been documented for overall health and injury prevention, however, studies have shown that a properly organized and setup work station can also increase productivity by up to 40%. Simple changes in desk height or keyboard positioning can decrease fatigue and strain, while organizing items that are most needed or used often into a reachable work space can decrease the amount of time and effort needed for each task. Oftentimes the changes needed to increase both your focus and productivity can be done in less than an hour, without any extra equipment.
>
> As a physical therapist working in a clinic dedicated to issues involving back and neck pain, I am constantly working with patients to find the right setup and position for their desk area or workspace, and in the past 5-10 years the

increased use of laptops and mobile devices has only accelerated the problem. Simply by taking the time to adjust their work stations, my clients have seen decreased levels of pain, fatigue, and stress while also reporting improved focus and productivity both at home and at work."

Sean Sumner MPT, OCS Lead Physical Therapist for the UC Davis Spine Center in Sacramento, California, and author of the Super Spine Series *available on Amazon*.

Ergonomically organised work space is not only about preventing injury or illness, but actually about improving productivity.

Not convinced yet? Try writing your report/assignment on a coffee table, or reading in a dark room. Not to mention messy desks, disorganised files, and disappearing office supplies.

Ergonomically organised work space is more than just making sure your desk is well lit and your chair comfy. It is also about organisation of your worktop, positioning of your computer, and other things.

Here is an example of an ergonomically set workspace:

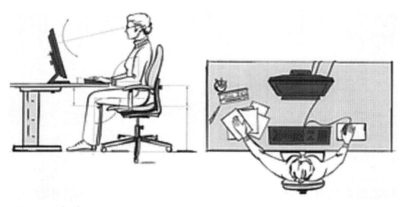

An example of an ergonomic workspace

1. How to Organise Your Desk/Work Surface

Let's start with **your desk**, or some other **work surface**.

Your desk, or table, or whatever surface you're using should support your key tasks, so it needs to be comfortable for whatever you do most often. For the majority of office workers, students, and other intellectually working souls, this will be writing, reading and computer-based tasks.

Your desk (and for the sake of simplifying things from now on, when I refer to 'your desk,' I also mean the table or some other work surface you use) should have a **height that suits your height** and **supports a good posture**. The idea is that you don't slouch or strain your neck or shoulders while working. The height of your desk should be comfortable for writing and typing.

How do you know that?

Sit at your workstation the way you usually do and do what you're supposed to be doing.

How long before you can feel some body discomfort?

If you can work fully concentrated for at least 60 minutes, without feeling any body discomfort, your workspace may be okay (but to double check, go over the points below to make sure your workspace is ergonomic).

But if your back is sore, your neck strained, your eyes itching, or you have any other body discomfort, you're likely to need to rearrange your workspace.

Here are a few steps to go through to ensure your workspace is ergonomic:

- **Adjust the height of your desk** if you can, but if not—don't despair— you can manipulate the height of your chair much more easily.
- **Adjust your chair**—see the picture above for some tips on the ideal position for your feet and the correct angles for your knees.
  Adjustable height chairs are very popular and you can get them at a reasonable price. If you have a fixed-height chair, you can try to adjust it with such DIY tricks as cushions for too low or footrests for too high seats. But if you plan to spend a lot of time at your workstation, focusing

on your work for long hours, getting a comfortable chair can help you maintain good posture and focus.

The ideal scenario is an ergonomic chair with adjustable seat height and adjustable backrest. The backrest should be set as far forward as possible, as the further back you put it, the more likely you are to slouch. Chairs with special support for your lower back are great, but expensive. A cheaper or free alternative is a rolled-up towel attached to the lower part of your backrest, or just a cushion/pillow tucked behind your lower back.

It's good to have armrests, too, and a cushion if your chair is hard.

Chairs that can swivel and roll will save you energy and time when reaching for stuff not within your immediate reach, so consider these features as well.

OPTIMISE YOUR WORKTOP/DESKTOP

The way our stuff is arranged on the desktop/worktop matters, too. You want to have stuff you use most often easy to reach and avoid unnecessary clutter.

Start with identifying your optimal viewing and normal reach zones.

Once you're sitting comfortably at your desk, pull up to the edges of your worktop and look ahead—what you can see is **your optimal viewing zone**. Everything you need for that particular working/study session should be within this zone and **nothing more!**

Then, reach each arm out to the side of your body and move across the desk until your hands meet in the middle, as if drawing a semi-circle just in front of you—**this is your normal reach zone**—this is where you should keep all the stuff you use most frequently.

The key message is that your desktop/worktop is for stuff that you require for this particular job you're doing right now, and nothing more.

Before you start every task, particularly more time-consuming tasks, or batches of similar tasks, think what you need to complete the task(s) and place it in your optimal viewing and normal reach zones. Everything else should be put away/hidden from view.

2. HOW TO POSITION YOUR COMPUTER/LAPTOP

- **Your keyboard and mouse** should be as close together as possible without getting in the way. Position the alphanumeric part—the one you use most often—right in front of your eyes. If you type a lot, think about the health of your wrists: ergonomics specialists advise placing the keyboard and mouse at the height that would not cause you to bend your wrists. Some people swear by mouse pads and keyboard wrist rests. I find it clunky, so check if it works for you.

- **Monitor**

  A well-positioned monitor is at an arm length away from you (so you can touch it from where you're sitting) and with the top 1/3 of your monitor at your eye level (see the picture). If it's not—there are multiple ways of adjusting the height of your monitor, ranging from special adjustable height stands to just tucking a couple of books under your monitor.

  Once you're done with the height, make sure there is no glare, checking the screen when lit with your usual source(s) of light—natural, as well as artificial.

3. HOW TO SET UP THE LIGHTING

Bad lighting can tire your eyes, and lead to dry or irritated eyes, which obviously can affect your ability to focus.

For general use, **glare-free, ambient light** should be okay. Use additional light for reading/writing or any other specific work requiring good lighting. Look for **low-glare, adjustable** lamps and position your lamp to the side of your computer, so that it illuminates your workspace but does not cause glare on your screen.

Mind the intensity of light—too much of it will cause the screen to appear 'washed out'. If you are using natural light, make sure you are positioned in a way that does not tire your eyes (e.g., light right into your eyes).

Watch out for direct light coming from windows as this can cause glare, too. Use blinds or curtains to control the amount of light, or if needed, change the position of your desk or your monitor.

4. MINIMISE NOISE

Noise is a **big distractor**, but often **underestimated**. Studies done on the effects of background noise ('ambient noise') at home, work, or school, show that even if unnoticed, this level of noise can affect our ability to concentrate, increasing stress levels and affecting our health. Sadly, humans do not habituate to noise, and the longer we continue to work in a noisy environment, the more it affects our ability to focus and our performance [2,3].

Sensitivity to noise is individual—some of us are more sensitive to it, some less. Many people find so-called white noise: undistinguishable, low-level background hums, murmurs, etc., helpful when trying to concentrate. Some people swear by 'focus-boosting' music. Find out what works best for you.

It's great if you are able to create a low-noise environment for your work/study. But often this is not possible, because it's out of your control. However, if your environment is noisy, you can still do something about it.

Here is a list of 'tools' you can try to see if it helps with noise:

- Noise-cancelling headphones
- Any headphones or earplugs
- Earphones/headphones with music (without lyrics, because lyrics usually create distractions by dragging us into the story or evoking memories) or white noise. You can find audio files with white noise or concentration-boosting music on the Net. Whatever you use, always make sure it helps you focus rather than distracts you.

TAKE CONTROL OF TECHNOLOGY BEFORE IT TAKES CONTROL OF YOU

Last but not least, the biggest killer of focus—technology

Technology can help you manage your time and productivity, but the reality is often different.

If you remember from Chapter 1: we have two types of attention, automatic and intentional. The automatic one is fine-tuned to detect any change in the environment as this may potentially mean 'Danger!' That's why automatic attention turns our focus to anything that flashes, pings, jumps, or makes any other sudden movement or appearance. And technology around us is designed to flash, ping, jerk, vibrate, ring...

That's why technology is becoming the number one killer of focus.

The truth is simple but brutal: if you want to improve your ability to concentrate on whatever you do, you must control the way you use technology and not let it control you.

Here are a few simple steps to help you regain control over your technological devices:

- Turn off notifications: email, social media, text messages, any updates (do your security updates before or at scheduled times). Generally speaking, anything that can make an unexpected appearance—whether visual or sound—can kill your focus. You can choose to have your notifications off at all times, or only at times of intense work.
  Set up specific times for checking and responding to your messages. Productivity gurus typically advise a limited number of checks/day, usually twice: once at the beginning and once at the end of the workday. If it's unrealistic for you, do whatever works for you. You can use your breaks, as long as it doesn't take more than a few minutes and is not too emotionally engaging, so you don't waste time and energy on calming down and refocusing when the break is over.
  Put your phone on silent or turn it off completely, unless you are expecting an important call. Let your messages go to the answering machine.

- If you decide to limit your access to email, phone, social media etc., it may be good to schedule a time when you attend to it and let people know about it. Record your own voicemail and 'out of office' messages, informing callers, emailers, etc., when you usually check your messages/emails. You may also want to set up 'an urgent access channel' (e.g., mobile phone) for all those messages that cannot wait until your next checking-in session and let people know about it (e.g., 'If this message is urgent, you can reach me at...').

- Limit the time you spend on the Internet
  This may sound obvious, but many people don't realise how much time they waste just browsing the Net or 'doing research.' Measuring how much time you spend on the Net can be quite enlightening and reinforce your decision to cut down on it.
  If you're struggling to resist the temptation of 'just one more quick look,' install access-blocking software (such as StayFocusd, LeechBlock, RescueTime, Self-control), or just turn off your Internet connection. Alternatively, try working in full screen mode (or use an app such as WriteRoom or Concentrate), or close any other applications.

- Put a limit on your research
  Whether you use the Internet or more traditional resources, the pursuit of information/knowledge can turn into a never-ending chase after 'the next shiny object' or the elusive 'perfect piece of evidence.' I tend to fall into that trap, too, so I've developed a system to limit the amount of time I spend:
  o I have a database of trustworthy sources bookmarked and try to stick to them
  o While gathering information, I take notes to monitor not only how much I've got, but also if I'm getting 'the same stuff' or any new information
  o I aim for a good range of quality sources, but when I see the same evidence or information being mentioned again, I know it's time to stop my research.

- Minimise the clutter on your screen/desktop

The same principles apply to your computer screen/desktop. Too much clutter can eat up a lot of time and distract you from what you should be doing.

First of all, don't have it all on your desktop. Yes, I have seen people have gazillions of icons on their desktops and struggle to find what they needed. Minimise the number of icons and shortcuts you keep handy.

Don't keep it all 'loose' in your Documents, either—group your documents into folders, ideally reflecting your filing system. Chose one method of organisation and stick with it. If you use two systems, electronic and paper, make sure you put the same names on the corresponding paper and electronic folders.

I have folders corresponding with the major projects: past and current. I also have folders where I put clippings, articles, and any other ideas related to projects I want to work on 'at some point in the future.'

If you use some sort of 'inbox' folder to hold all those documents and other matters that still need to be dealt with, move the documents to the appropriate folder as soon as you have dealt with it, or at specified clean-up times. I use Desktop for all those current/open tasks.

Work in a full screen mode, or use apps that simulate it (e.g. StayFocusd, LeechBlock, RescueTime, Self-Control).

Timothy Kenny has an excellent system to help him organise his workload.

"The Key to Focus: Isolate Your Roles

It's hard to stay focused when you have a bunch of different projects competing for your time. Here's how I keep it all organized.

I split up everything I do into one of 4 main categories. Those are Career, Personal, Relationships, and Health. There is also a fifth category, which is a meta-level, which is meant to organize and integrate the 4 main categories.

Each day of the week I focus on one category. Monday is Career, Tuesday is Relationships, Wednesday is Health, Thursday is Personal, and Friday is the Meta category.

For each day, I have a different set of bookmarks that I check in my browser. I create a folder of bookmarks for each day of the week, and on each day I open the bookmarks for that day and do a check-up.

When I have to shift into a role for a special activity, like teaching a course, I create a whole different user account on my computer. This helps me keep my desktop organized so that there are only shortcuts to the programs and folders I need for that role.

Other roles include video editing, music production, and web design.

Any major role you have can become its own user account. By keeping things separate, you increase your focus and efficiency while taking on each role. Instead of trying to block out the 90% of "stuff" that isn't relevant to your current role, you can switch to a new account that shows you just the tool you need to get the job done.

Get started now... think of one major role you have outside of your day-to-day activities, and create a second user account just for that activity.

1. Delete everything on the desktop except the programs and folders you really need.

2. Find a high quality wallpaper image that represents that role and set it as your desktop background.

3. Find an image you can use for the user profile image.

All set...you're ready to go!"

Timothy Kenny
Author of *"Accelerated Learning for Entrepreneurs"*
www.TimothyKenny.com

In this chapter I've explained the importance of an ergonomically organised workspace and given you tips on setting it up. You also know how to minimise noise and take control of technology.

In the next chapter, we will explore how to optimise your body for maximum cognitive performance (and focus, of course).

CHAPTER 6 -
OPTIMISE YOUR BODY
TO MAX OUT YOUR COGNITIVE POWERS

This chapter zooms in on your body. Why? Because there are close connections between our body and our mind. We may not know exactly how it all works together, but we've been exploring that from ancient times. Hippocrates and his followers made the first attempts to understand the complex connections between mental and physiological processes. Ancient Romans had a motto: *Mens sana in corpore sano*—A sane mind in a sound body. Throughout history, doctors, scientists, and philosophers have been trying to explain those connections. Although there are still some unknowns, science can now tell us what aspects of our body and physiological processes influence learning, thinking, and memory.

I will show you how you can improve your mental performance and your focus in particular by addressing the following aspects:

- Ergonomics of your body
- A good night's sleep
- Breaks
- Nutrition
- Exercise

First, let's look at how you can improve the ergonomics of your body for better cognitive performance.

If you're reading this chapter, it's likely your Distraction Logs highlighted that your body can get in the way of your focus.

How often do signals from your body get through to you and disrupt your attempts to focus? What is it? What distracts you most often?

The most common causes for your body to scream for attention are:

- Uncomfortable position, aches and pain, particularly within the back area
- Tiredness, which is usually due to insufficient rest, whether in the form of breaks or the night's rest/sleep
- Hunger, or more precisely, low blood glucose levels
- Low energy, which may be the result of low glucose level, or an overall sense of sluggishness or lethargy.

Let's look at some solutions to those problems, now.

HOW TO PREVENT BACK PAIN AND OTHER PROBLEMS WITH UNCOMFORTABLE POSITION

Back pain and strain injuries are one of the most common workplace problems. Aches and pains from your uncomfortable body—whether it's your back, neck, wrists or feet—are hard to ignore, too. Ironically, I had some neck pain while writing this chapter (a strain from having to work at a badly designed workstation the day before) and it disrupted my work process considerably—I had to get up and stretch every few minutes.

It pays to make sure that your workstation (desk, table, work surface) is designed in an ergonomic way, adapted to your specific needs. For tips on how to create an ergonomic workspace, check Chapter 5.

HOW TO DEAL WITH TIREDNESS

To paraphrase the ancient proverb quoted above, in a tired body, the spirit is tired, too. We need rest in order to function, and our brain is one of the reasons why we need down time.

Two main aspects of rest and restoration when it comes to work, and intellectual work in particular, are:

- Sleep, which is crucial for learning and memory formation
- Breaks, which are important to keep up good concentration.

In a nutshell, in order to be able to focus, we need to sleep and take breaks.

Let's look at how to do it now.

SLEEP

I'm sure you know that sleep deprivation affects your level of alertness and hence your ability to focus. Simply speaking, in order to be able to think, read, listen to stuff, process information and remember it, your brain needs a decent amount of sleep. During sleep, our brain goes over the neural pathways created during learning and 'practice,' strengthening what we have learnt that day, whether it is study material, new foreign vocabulary, or how to operate that fancy new tablet or an app.

74

Sleep deprivation also affects your judgement, ability to concentrate, think, and carry out many tasks.

How much sleep do we need?

An average adult, according to the National Sleep Foundation [1], needs 7-9 hours of sleep per night. Some people can function on less, some need more. Anything less than 6 hours is not recommended and can be dangerous, particularly for a prolonged period of time (if your sleep does not fall within the normal limits, or you have any other problems with your sleep, you should talk to your doctor about it).

Acute sleep deprivation and its effects on your ability to focus, learn, and work are often obvious. One sleepless night impairs our performance as much as having 0.10% of alcohol in your blood (above legal driving limits in any country).

But people who suffer from chronic sleep debt often get used to these states (habituate) and hence they may feel like they can function well intellectually. Sadly, more often than not, their judgement of their ability to attend to mental tasks requiring attention, concentration and good memory are often impaired (they rate themselves higher than they actually perform).

If you don't sleep as much as you should, you create 'sleep debt,' which, like any other debt, accumulates and need to be 'paid off.'

What's the price of not 'paying off' your sleep debt? There are multiple costs, some of them quite dangerous, including impaired coordination or sleepiness when operating machinery or driving. And many of them affect your concentration and other 'mental powers.'

So if you are suffering from:

- Forgetfulness
- Working memory lapses
- Confusion
- Impaired attention
- Irritability

You may need to look at how much sleep you have had over the last few days and make sure you can catch up on your 'zzz' as soon as you can.

How to improve your sleep?

- Be mindful of how much you sleep. Keep a diary, if you need to.
- Make a resolution to go to bed earlier, or let yourself sleep in when possible.
- In crunch times (e.g., exam time, an important project with pressing deadline), if you have to work long hours/stay up late, consider 'recharging' during the day with power naps. Power naps are short, 15-20 minute naps designed to 'reset your brain.'
- The key to success with power naps is not to fall into a deep sleep and avoid starting a sleep cycle that you are not able to complete, and which will cause you to wake up feeling groggy, drowsy, and anything but mentally sharp. You may need to do some testing to determine what your optimal length of nap is, but as a rule of thumb, anything longer than 30 minutes increases the risk of waking up feeling groggy. Set your alarm. Use quiet rooms, eye masks and make sure you are warm enough to increase your chances of restorative sleep [2].
- Use **sleep hygiene** advice for better sleep (you can find good sleep hygiene advice on the National Sleep Foundation Website [3]—you will find the link in the Resources Section.

Breaks

Breaks are important, too, not only to prevent tiredness, but also to maintain focus.

If you remember from Chapter 1, we can focus on something intentionally for about 10 minutes. Obviously, taking a break every 10 minutes is not practical, however pushing on for too long is not good for our mental performance either.

Nathaniel Kleitman, a sleep researcher, discovered that [4] we operate in 90-minute cycles of activity and rest, during the night and day. This phenomenon has been called ultradian rhythm by other researchers.

Tony Schwartz, the author of *The Way We're Working Isn't Working*, and many other productivity experts, recommends working in 60-90 minute periods [5] to maximise on this rhythm.

I have tried it too, and I admit I tend to last around 60 minutes before I need to get up and stretch or just walk around for a couple of minutes. It's because I think best when I'm moving, and because my back needs a break more often.

Overall, as with anything, I recommend you find your own 'sweet spot,' testing the length of your optimal focus period before you take a break. But as a rule of thumb, do not exceed 90 minutes.

HERE ARE SOME SUGGESTIONS FOR HOW TO TAKE AN EFFECTIVE BREAK:

- **Take short** (about 5 minute) **breaks every 60-90 minutes**; get up and move around. Don't get engaged in any activity requiring intellectual effort (your brain is running low on productivity) or may result in emotional states (you don't want to waste time trying to calm down afterwards). Light, mundane tasks, such as some house chores or making yourself a cup of tea, are perfect.

- **Take a longer (20-30 minute) break every 2-3hours**; you can use it for a quick (snack) or longer (lunch) meal. Change of scenery and some movement work well here. If you're working long days, you may want to use one of your longer breaks for exercise.

- Breaks are for recharging, so don't do any important work or any work-related activities when on a break.
  The key here is not to initiate any activity that would engage you emotionally, mentally, or overtly physically, so you don't have to then calm yourself or otherwise waste time to refocus. So, avoid emotionally difficult conversations with your nearest and dearest, or phone calls to that lousy customer service that hasn't responded to your complaint, or water cooler chats with a colleague you don't like.

- If you've got a problem with short attention span, and display other symptoms of ADHD or ADD, you may need to consult your doctor/health practitioner. However, if you're otherwise healthy but struggling to extend your focus beyond that 10 minutes' mark, check Chapter 10 for more suggestions on how to improve your attention span.

HOW TO EAT FOR OPTIMUM COGNITIVE PERFORMANCE

In order to work fast, your brain needs a steady supply of ready-to-use fuel.

Why?

Because the brain's job is to think, not to process food. And also, the brain does not have any 'food storage capacity.'

The fuel in this case is glucose.

In practice, the brain utilizes about 120g of glucose, or 420kcal (1760kJ) per day, irrespective of how much thinking or learning we are doing [6].

The tricky bit is that the supply of the fuel needs to be steady.

Why?

Because both a drop and a high in blood glucose can have a negative effect on the ability to concentrate.

A drop in glucose levels in your blood, even if you are overall healthy, is likely to make you feel tired, nervous, restless and unable to concentrate and think clearly. On the other hand, a sudden spike in blood glucose is not good for your brain either. A snack high in carbs or a sweet drink can give you an initial boost in energy, but this peak in glucose level in your blood will be quickly brought down by insulin (assuming you don't have any metabolic/diabetic problems), resulting in another low. You're likely to go searching for another 'sugar fix,' resulting in another sugar high and subsequent low. This yo-yo effect, although it may initially help you to focus, is not good for longer-term work and your overall health.

What you eat and how you eat is important to effective focus and other mental capabilities. Read on to learn more about focus-enhancing nutrition.

HERE ARE SOME SUGGESTIONS FOR 'FOCUS-BOOSTING' NUTRITION

1. EAT 'BRAIN FRIENDLY FOOD'

As I said above, brain food is simple and plain glucose. It's practically the only nutrient our brain is able to use. Without any 'food storage capacity,' the brain needs a continuous supply of glucose. But glucose is a simple sugar and disappears quickly from our bloodstream. So we need to eat something that would release glucose in a continuous way without harmful highs and lows.

How can you ensure your brain is 'fed' appropriately?

By eating so called 'brain friendly' food:

- Complex carbohydrates (complex sugars) are great for providing slow-release glucose. Foods in this group include: grains and whole-grain breads and pastry, starchy vegetables such as potatoes, corn, and pulses (beans, peas, lentils).

- Proteins are also important, although not a direct source of brain food.

- Fats are a rich source of energy that is slowly released, so it acts as storage in times of starvation. Omega-3 fatty acids, present in some fish (mackerel, herring, tuna, salmon) and nuts, may help improve concentration and academic ability.

- Antioxidants—nutrients of various kinds, whose main role is to get rid of free radicals, which damage brain cells. Foods rich in antioxidants are berries, cherries, citrus and other fruits, and vegetables, such as spinach, broccoli, carrots, some herbs and spices (onion, garlic, cinnamon, basil), and some kids of tea (green and white).

2. Avoid 'Brain unfriendly' food

- Simple sugars (simple carbohydrates) such as sweets, biscuits, fruit juice, and jams are like an injection of fuel that causes a temporary boost in energy, but is used up or stored away (by insulin) quickly and causes a low—not good.
- Junk food is not only calorie-rich and nutrition poor, but also rich in saturated trans fats, which are considered to have adverse effect on cognition.

3. Be smart about how you eat

How to eat is as important as what to eat when it comes to brain-friendly nutrition. As we already know, the key to a steady intellectual 'workout' is a steady supply of glucose.

- Eating 3 meals a day, even if well balanced, still creates three spikes of 'glucose highs' in our system, leading to lows a couple of hours after the meal.
- A morning and afternoon tea, or a small snack, should keep the blood glucose levels steady. It's best to eat something with complex carbs and some protein to keep a steady supply of glucose for the brain. A grain & nuts bar, low-fat yoghurt with muesli, or a slice of wholemeal bread with cheese should keep us going until the next meal.

4. What about caffeine and other 'mental enhancers'?

Now, a quick note on the effects of caffeine (and some energy drinks) on cognitive performance (and hence focus). Many people look for some magic potion that would instantly improve their mental powers. And while researches and marketers (more the latter than the former) keep coming up with the new magic potions or devices, those 'magic cures' are more likely to be another hype rather than bring actual, repeatable and measurable results.

Don't get me wrong, I would love to know that magic trick which will improve my memory and ability to learn and think clearly. But judging by the state of science today, we still have some work to do.

Below is a short summary of current evidence behind some commonly used LEGAL non-prescription substances. Check the Resources section for suggestions on where to find more details.

CAFFEINE

There is an extensive body of research on the effects of caffeine on physical and mental performance. The results are not as powerful as some coffee lovers may wish. Here is a summary of a number of studies I have sifted through [9, 10]:

Caffeine in moderate amounts in healthy, non-pregnant adult individuals:

- Can delay fatigue during exercise/physical activity by increasing energy availability and decreasing the sense of effort needed for the activity
- (Usually) improves reaction time
- Does not usually affect long-term memory, but may have positive or negative effects on short term (working) memory
- Facilitates learning in tasks in which information is presented passively (e.g., you're watching an educational video or listening to a podcast/book), but has no effect in tasks where material is learned intentionally (e.g., you trying to find a solution to your problem)
- Appears to improve our working memory when we're tired or sleep deprived and in lighter tasks.
- At low doses, improves mood and reduces anxiety, while at high doses, there is an increase in tense arousal, including anxiety, nervousness, and jitteriness, which subsequently impact cognitive performance indirectly
- Caffeine may have a negative effect on sleep, resulting in daytime sleepiness

ENERGY DRINKS

There is a wide variety of energy drinks available on the market. They all contain a number of ingredients for which very little information is available.

Overall, the evidence is not strong or conclusive enough regarding their effects on mental and physical performance [11], and there appear to be considerable risks associated with their use/abuse particularly when used with alcohol [11] and for young people [12]. I do not use them personally and do not recommend using—apply your own good judgement.

5. Boost your cognitive performance with exercise

I guess you probably already know how exercise can benefit our physical and mental health, but boosting cognitive performance? Really?

Yes, really. Exercise boosts our cognitive performance and there is plenty of evidence to support that.

In his fantastic book *Brain Rules* [7], John Medina, a developmental molecular biologist, presents unshakable evidence of the impact of exercise on our ageing, memory, executive functions and many other 'cognitive powers.'

'The brain appears to be designed to solve problems related to surviving in an unstable outdoor environment, and to do so in nearly constant motion.'

I encourage you to read John Medina's book—it's life changing. It has definitely changed mine. I read it at the time when I was really struggling to function intellectually and creatively. I was going through a personal crisis and really needed to be at the top of my game, only to find that—my brain was failing me.

I felt constantly tired, overworked, and struggled to get stuff done. In an attempt to improve my well-being, I started cutting down on my commitments, limited my social engagements, said no to some new opportunities and started sleeping more, which helped to some extent. Yet, I was still feeling tired, to the point I was feeling too tired to walk to and from work, so I started using my car and more convenient buses. To my unpleasant surprise, it did not help much, and worse, my cognitive performance started to spiral down. I was catching myself sitting at my laptop, staring at an email or an article and really struggling to understand what it all meant. My memory was getting really poor, to the point I thought that maybe I was developing early dementia.

At that time, I was working on one of my video courses (Crack Your Learning Code—Learn Faster. Remember for Longer) and wanted to jam pack it with up-to date scientific evidence, so I picked up *Brain Rules* by John Medina. But as I was going through the chapters, I discovered that my lifestyle was far from 'brain friendly.'

This was an eye-opening read. It made me realise that by not exercising, however tired I felt, I was actually further impairing my intellectual performance.

Following the enlightening evidence Medina presents, I started making changes in my lifestyle, even though it felt a little counterintuitive at times. The most powerful effect was created by regular exercise: my memory improved, my creative thinking blossomed again, and on top of that, my mood and ability to cope with stress also got better. I have been running regularly ever since, and if I happen to not be able to run for longer than a couple of weeks, I can see how my ability to think clearly and remember things slips back.

In a nutshell, Medina quoted multiple studies, spread across ages and stages, but the evidence is clear: people who led active lifestyles performed better at tasks such as long-term memory, reasoning, attention, problem-solving, executive function, spatial tasks, reaction times and quantitative skills than those with sedentary lifestyles.

Moreover, if you start exercising regularly, your cognitive powers improve. And they go down again to the pre-exercise levels when you stop.

What does it mean?

Exercise is the cheapest and easiest cognitive enhancer available.

Exercise boots our cognitive performance by increasing the oxygen flow into the brain and by boosting the creation, survival, and resistance of brain cells.

Sedentary lifestyles are likely to lead to cognitive decline, no matter what age.

So how much exercise should we do? How often? What kind?

I am not an exercise or fitness expert, but from what I found out, in a nutshell, the amount and type of exercise depends, and it varies individually.

First of all, your exercise routine needs to be adapted to your current fitness level and your overall health. Don't try to go straight into the 'doing a half marathon' mode. If you are not exercising much right now, you may need to build up your fitness level slowly, gradually. There is lots of advice on what to do and how to do it out there. If you have any health concerns or doubts, seek advice from your doctor.

Studies show that 30 minutes 2-3 times per week of aerobic exercise (running, brisk walking, swimming, etc.) can help boost your cognitive powers; adding a strengthening program to it will further improve it.

Remember, individual effects vary. Please consult your doctor before embarking on any serious, rigorous exercise.

But don't overdo it, either. Too much exercise and exhaustion can hurt cognition.

In this chapter, we explored ways of improving your cognitive performance, and your focus in particular, by helping your body function at the top of the game. We discussed how you can boost your mental powers through improving the ergonomics of your posture, good sleep, effective breaks, 'brain friendly' nutrition, and exercise. In the next chapter, I will walk you through strategies for managing your mind for a laser-sharp focus.

CHAPTER 7 -
MANAGE YOUR MIND
FOR A LASER-SHARP FOCUS

Disclaimer: The author is not an expert in any of the areas discussed in this chapter. The information in this book is intended for educational and informational purposes and applies to adult, non-pregnant, non-breastfeeding healthy individuals and should not be treated as advice. All attempts have been made to verify the information provided in this chapter, but the author does not assume any responsibility for errors, omissions or contrary interpretations of the subject matter herein. Neither the author nor the publisher assumes any responsibility for any specific health needs that may require medical supervision or attention, and is not liable for negative consequences from actions resulting from reading or following the information provided in this chapter. If you have any specific questions about any medical or nutritional matter, consult your doctor or other healthcare provider. It has been compiled from medically-reviewed websites (see Resource section for more details). It is not meant to, and should not be used to diagnose or substitute for medical advice and treatment. You must not rely on this information as an alternative to seeking advice from your healthcare provider. If you have any specific questions about any mental and emotional problems, consult your doctor or other healthcare provider. Seek immediate medical attention if you think you may be suffering from any medical or mental health condition. Never delay seeking medical advice, disregard medical advice or discontinue treatment because of the information provided below.

In this chapter we will look at focus problems that originate from your mind. The most common of those internal stimuli are thoughts and emotions.

If you came to this chapter following advice from the Laser-Sharp Focus Roadmap, then you're already aware of what your mind-bound problems are. However, if you lack this clarity, I'd urge you to run a Distraction Log for a few days and analyse the results. The clearer you are on what's getting in the way of your focus, the more targeted your intervention will be, and hence the more effective.

How to Manage Your Emotions and Use Them for a More Powerful Memory

Have you ever tried focusing on reading your textbook just before your exam, or when you had an exciting date in a couple of hours? And what about attending a presentation on the day of your first product launch—how much do you remember from it? I wouldn't be surprised if, unless you repeated the reading or listened to the presentation again at a later date, you did not remember much. Anxiety, excitement and anticipation probably took over your ability to pay full attention and learn.

Focus can only happen if you're able to be in control of your mind and can direct your attention to concentrate on the chosen thing.

Emotions are powerful. They can take over your mind and flood you with equally powerful physiological effects, resulting in you being taken over by whatever your emotional mind is dictating. In order to be receptive to focus, you need to be in control of your mind.

You may have heard of 'rational' mind and 'emotional' mind or thinking. To focus, you need your rational, cool, analytical, decision-making mind well in control. In order to achieve that, you need to manage your emotional side: impulsive, energetic, keen to take action.

If you want to be able to focus at any time, for a decent length of time, you need to be able to control your emotions.

Emotions are very important when it comes to concentration and focus. Why?

Because emotions attract our attention. We pay attention to anything that's emotional, negatively or positively: joy, happiness, fear or anger.

Emotions can hold sway over our ability to focus. Positive as much as negative, they can seriously play with your mind and diminish your ability to think, process information and concentrate.

There is another, sneakier way emotions can drive your attention away from what you should be doing.

Emotions are like shiny, colourful buttons on the grey, boring fabric of our mundane reality. If you are working on something monotonous and dry, your attention is likely to fall for something more colourful and lively (like all those cute animal videos on Facbook). The reward is immediate: joy, happiness, or even fear and anger, unlike the postponed reward from getting your job done.

Your search for emotional stimulation can fuel procrastination.

On the other hand, as I said above, we pay attention to anything that is emotional. That means emotions can enhance our ability to be attentive and remember. The trick is to find that sweet spot where your emotional state enhances rather than hinders your cognitive powers.

HOW TO MANAGE EMOTIONS SO THAT THEY DON'T GET IN THE WAY OF YOUR FOCUS (PREVENTATIVELY)

If you find yourself being overwhelmed by your emotional state, be it a stressful situation in your professional or personal life, an illness, a happy event on the horizon or some other difficult time, here are a few techniques I researched and/or personally tried in time of emotional difficulty:

I. LEAVE YOUR WORK IN YOUR OFFICE, AND HOME TROUBLE AT HOME

Develop a habit of leaving any stresses, problems or other emotionally charged thoughts where they belong. I suggest doing it even for happy events—take the energy and positive feeling with you, but try to leave the content, so that it does not distract you.

How to do it:

- Try visualising that when you are closing/locking the door, you leave all the emotionally charged events behind that door
- Use the journey to and from as a clear divider: make it about 'the in-between time.' Don't allow yourself to dwell on what's happened, don't revisit the conversations, don't replay events.
- Focus on something neutral that doesn't belong to either of the spaces you are traveling between (e.g., read a book/paper; listen to music/podcasts; you can also have topic you want to think of, such as planning your holidays, or your next blog post)

2. AIR YOUR HEAD

This works well in combination with number 1 on this list.

Personally, I find walking an excellent way to clear my head and leave things (particularly work) behind. Many of the professional helpers I spoke to identify the importance of using the journey home to create a strong work/home boundary.

Set up your from-work journey in a way that has some walking included. If you can't walk all the way, try walking at least a little. Get on your bus/train one stop farther, or off it one stop earlier, and walk the remaining distance. Park your car at the farthest end. Take the stairs instead of the lift. You can practice 'leaving your work behind' strategies described above while doing it.

Walking works best, because of the added bonus of exercise and being out there in the real world, ideally in nature. But if you can't walk, whether you're driving, using public transport or a passenger in someone else' car, make sure you are deliberately using the commute time to air your head. Light readings, listening to positive music or non-work related conversations all can help.

3. SLEEP AND SLEEP IT OFF WHEN NEEDED

Sleep is necessary for processing of learning and anything else that happens to us during the day. This is when all those (important for effective learning and memory formation) connections between brain cells are formed. Sleep deprivation reduces our ability to cope with emotions, as any new parents can attest. By making sure you sleep adequately, you reduce the risk of letting your emotions take over your mind.

I also use sleep/naps to manage particularly emotionally stressful states. Short naps after a particularly emotionally charged day have been my most effective strategy for 'resetting' my brain when I have something important I need to focus on later that day and the above strategies have not worked.

Because of the conditioning to 'it's a new day... I can start afresh,' my brain helps me put whatever has happened behind me, even with a short nap. I usually take a power nap of 15- 20 minutes, making sure it's no longer than that, and wake up with my mind 'wiped clean' so I can start afresh. If you really need more sleep, just go to bed early.

4. SLOW DOWN AND DOWNSIZE

This is not a quick fix but more of a lifestyle habit. If you find yourself often emotionally affected by stuff, take time to reflect what is really important in your life. Do it regularly, make sure you prioritise accordingly. Once you have clarity in the life priorities department, try to eliminate what is not essential. Slow down, learn to say 'no' to all those unimportant, emotionally draining things. Consider reducing the amount of time spent watching TV, using social media, or socialising (particularly with toxic people). You may be surprised to discover how much of your emotional clutter is actually not even yours.

5. DO AN 'EMOTIONAL DUMP' BEFORE YOU SIT DOWN TO DO YOUR WORK

Many people find that 'getting it off their chest' helps them leave their emotional ballast behind. If you need to clear your mind from emotional effects of the day, try 'dumping' it. This is not about asking for advice or support. It is plainly about 'getting it off your chest.'

How to do it?

- Talk to someone you trust, but ask them just to listen, not to comment. Be clear and honest about explaining the point of this exercise and ask your friend/partner if this would be okay with them. Remember, it's not about seeking help or support, or worse, getting into an argument about what's happened.

This technique can only work if both you and your friend/partner can refrain from commenting or entering any kind of conversation.

As with any other technique I suggest, try it and see if it works for you. I know people who find this strategy helpful, but I have tried it and did not like it. Even when I managed to find someone who would just listen without trying to give me advice or emotional support, I did not like 'reliving' the experience when telling about it.

- Journal:
  This is a great way of doing a 'dump' without bothering anyone. As long as you can keep it focused on getting it off your chest, it should be 'short and sweet.' Try doing it without censoring your thoughts. Write about your feelings just as they are. Some people prefer to do 'stream of consciousness' journaling, some prefer a more reflective approach. If you have a preference, go for it. If not, find out what works for you.

> **Warning!** The point is not so much discussing the matter, but doing a 'dump.' The distinction is quite important, because there are things that you may want and really should discuss with your nearest and dearest, to seek their advice or support. Here, we are talking about all those things that are not really that important, but keep bugging you or cluttering your mind. Having an 'emotional dump' may help you clear it.

Be mindful, though, for some people, revisiting those 'don't really want to be bothered by' events and irritations is counterproductive as it only reminds them of the events and brings them to the fore. Check to see if it works for you, and don't do it if it doesn't.

HOW TO REGAIN CONTROL OF YOUR MIND WHEN EMOTIONS TAKE OVER

The techniques described above are best used as 'preventive strategies.' Use them on a regular basis for a better sense of control over your emotional mind. However, if you find yourself being distracted by your emotional state right in the middle of something, here are a couple of things you can try to bring your mind back to focus.

1. Breathe and refocus

If you find yourself distracted by your thoughts or emotional remnants of earlier events, just take a deep breath and refocus on whatever you are trying to do. Rinse and repeat, focusing on your breathing. Then switch your focus back to your task.

2. Have your own grounding trick to refocus

I wrote elsewhere in the book about little tricks you can use to bring yourself back into focus. These little techniques originate from anxiety management and sensory modulation and are very effective in bringing your focus back into the here and now.

Over the years, I have developed a toolkit of grounding tricks, inspired by multiple therapeutic approaches (for a full list of resources check the Resources section of this book). Below are a few of my favourites, together with what other people I've worked with found helpful. Pick these one by one and test them to see if they work for you. Don't worry if one strategy does not work for you—give it some time (try for at least a few days). If this one doesn't work, try another one. It's good to have a few tricks up your sleeve, so don't stop experimenting.

The mechanisms behind those techniques is to cut through your mental noise/clutter with sensory input, that is, by using your vision, hearing, touch, smell, taste. We all have different sensory preferences, so again, see whatever works for you.

- Use your eyes:
  Notice and name 5 things around you
  Blink 10 times
  Look around yourself and find 5 things in your favourite colour

- Use your hearing:
  Say something out loud, e.g., count backward, say your name; I often say out loud whatever the last word on my mind was

- Smell:
  Notice the smells around you, go and sniff a lemon/a flower/your favourite perfume (some people keep a little collection of essential oils)

- Taste:
  Make yourself a cup of tea/coffee and sip on it when you feel distracted; savour the taste

- Touch:
  Touch your hand/chair/desk, notice the texture, etc., and remind yourself you have something to focus on

- Physical activity:
  Stretch, wave your hand, wear a rubber band on your wrist and snap lightly when you want to refocus

2. ACKNOWLEDGE AND MOVE ON—PRACTICE MINDFULNESS AND MEDITATION

A great way to master your emotional states is practicing mindfulness and meditation. Studies show that mindfulness reduces our tendency to ruminate on stuff, helps us focus and disengage from emotionally upsetting thoughts, boosts our working memory—the list goes on. [1] There are lots of fantastic resources on 'how to' out there. Check the Resources section for some suggestions.

Remember, mindfulness does not require you to sit down in a special space—you can do it anywhere at any time. You can also combine it with other techniques mentioned above—I do it on my way home from work, while walking, and sometimes in micro doses when having breathe-and-refocus moments.

USE YOUR EMOTIONS FOR POWERFUL MEMORY

On the flip side—emotions are what we remember. Emotions are like little tags 'Remember me!' for our brain. That's why emotions can be incredibly helpful in anything that requires memory: whether it's memorising historical dates, learning new vocabulary, or practicing your presentation.

Strangely enough, it does not really matter much whether these are positive or negative emotions, because both types can help you remember, as long as they are at the optimal level of intensity and duration at the time.

If you read about the effect of 'too much for too long' stress in the previous chapter, you will not be surprised to hear that research shows experiencing too many emotions, positive or negative, or emotions going on for too long will overwhelm us.

Why?

Because with too much emotion we lose focus. It's hard to ignore that paralysing fear, overwhelming sadness or boundless joy. Let that feeling in and you're struggling to concentrate on your task.

How much is just enough? How long is just right? Ideally, you want something to last as long as the study/work session you need it for. If not the whole, then at least a part of it.

As for the intensity of your emotional state—there is a level of emotional response or emotional arousal that enhances cognitive processes. It's hard to quantify it, but you can easily find out what works for you by experimenting with various levels of your emotional response until you find your 'sweet spot.'

How to use emotions for better focus

I. Make your work/learning emotionally appealing

You can achieve it by using things such as visual aids ('pretty, shiny things'), or using other senses (e.g., nice-smelling study room). I strongly believe that one of the reasons why I have been so persistent with my morning study/work routine is a cup of coffee. I program the coffee machine so that I wake up to the smell of freshly brewing coffee. And man, this is a smell I want to get up to, even when I don't have to (e.g., on weekends).

Use little sensory tricks like that.

2. Spice it up with (a little) stress

A little stress can motivate us to push on in the rush to the finish line.

A looming deadline, exam anxiety, fear of failure or desire to fulfil a promise made to someone can power our ability to focus. However, too much stress can kill it.

The key is to find that 'sweet spot' of so-called optimal emotional arousal: enough to light the fire, but not enough to burn you out.

Use deadlines to help you motivate yourself. Deadlines create a sense of urgency and a challenge: will I get there on time? Many people like having tight deadlines—having a clear sense of something hanging over your head may make you push on a little harder.

- Use deadlines you are given, such as assignment/report due dates, exams, monthly performance meetings, etc. to drive your motivation
- Create your own deadlines if you don't have any given, but also when the given deadlines are too far in the future. Keep it close enough for the sense of urgency, but realistic.

Beware! The flip side of using deadlines as motivators is waiting until the deadline is really looming, e.g., leaving revision to the night before the exam is due or starting to write your report on the morning it's due. This approach can result in poor quality or unfinished work and extra, unnecessary stress for you.

- Use social obligations to increase the stakes
  Having some sort of social obligation to fulfil, whether is it in collaboration or in competition with someone, can also give you that extra push.
  o Team up with someone/find an accountability buddy and check in with them regularly to report on your progress
  o Offer to present your work (or part of it) to a group of co-workers for feedback before the job is actually due. Or, if your work can benefit anyone else in the organisation/team, your study group, or your fellow co-founders, volunteer to prepare a presentation or write a summary report for them

For more tips on how to use and manage stress, see Chapter 12.

3. Design your own system of rewards

Use little extrinsic motivators to boost your drive to the finish line. Be careful not to kill your intrinsic motives (see Chapter 4 for more details), but make sure you care about those rewards. You can promise yourself your favourite snacks, or time spent procrastinating on your favourite game, or whatever you fancy. Keep an eye on the proportions, so that consuming your rewards doesn't take over your work time.

4. Make your motivation for your goals emotional

Extrinsic or intrinsic, positive or negative, emotions can be powerful motivators. When you formulate your goals and explore your motivation (Chapters 3 and 4), make sure you have at least a couple of emotional reasons WHY. For example, your goal of graduating from college/university or completing a project may be that it will give you a sense of achievement and pride. If you're setting up a business from home, you're likely to be looking for independence and happiness in work/life balance.

5. Put yourself in the mood for work

- Set up your work/study environment to enhance the sense of joy or slight stress (remember the 'sweet spot' rule: not too much and not for too long)
- Experiment with various moods: negative emotions, such as fear or anger can help enhance our analytical functions, critical thinking and attention to detail. Positive emotions such as joy, happiness and pride can boost creative, outside-the-box approaches. When in doubt, go for the positive emotions.
- Use some 'aids,' such as doing something that makes you laugh or smile before your study session. When I'm in a need of an emotional booster before a work session, I watch funny videos on YouTube or look up LOL Cats. But for you it may be playing with your pet, listening to your favourite song, or chatting to someone you like/love.
- Do something that makes you feel accomplished and successful, even if it's washing a pile of dishes.

6. MANAGE TOO-POWERFUL EMOTIONS

However, if you find yourself in a situation outside your 'sweet spot' and your emotional state is getting in the way of your concentration, don't let it overwhelm you completely. Try strategies described in **How to regain control of your mind when emotions take over section** to regain control of your mind.

HOW TO MANAGE FREE-RANGE THOUGHTS, BURSTS OF IDEAS, AND OTHER CHALLENGES OF A WANDERING MIND

Do you find yourself juggling many thoughts, ideas or to-dos at the same time? Does your mind have a mind of its own and keep wandering off when you should be focusing on the job at hand? Do you feel that your mind is like a big, crowded office with lots of half-open files with bits and pieces of paper slipping out of it, laying scattered around, hanging off walls...?

If this is what your mind feels like, you are not alone. I've been there, many times. I even used to pride myself on being able to stay on top of that mess, knowing where stuff was, remembering lots of little details and being able to recall a multi-layered novel plot I developed years ago. As I grew older and busier, I started forgetting more and more, including people's names, birthdays, and even my own address.

What saved me from despair was David Allen's book and time management system *Getting Things Done (GTD)*. You can learn more about it from his fantastic book: *Getting Things done: The Art of Stress-Free Productivity*, and his website http://gettingthingsdone.com/ [2]

I adapted some of the GTD processes, added a few techniques from psychological and cognitive neuroscience baskets, and came up with the system for managing a wandering mind as described below.

STEP 1: DECLUTTER YOUR MIND

Just as you would do with a real messy office, to keep your mind organised and on track, start with decluttering it.

This is one of the most powerful GTD techniques. All you need is pen and paper (or a suitable piece of software) to capture all those free-range thoughts. Better still, set up an 'idea notebook' so you can keep your ideas in one place.

This strategy works great as an initial 'mind clean-up,' but can improve your productivity further when done on regular basis.

Here is how you can go about it:

- Offload on the paper all the thoughts you're holding in your head at the moment
- Write one thought/idea per line, so that you can clearly see the separation

Once you've got your thoughts out on the piece of paper, you can either leave it there and get on with your job, knowing your great ideas are safe and you can come back to them whenever you want to, or move on to the next step: coding and filing it (this is good if you are doing this exercise as an initial clean-up).

STEP 2: HAVE A SYSTEM FOR CAPTURING YOUR FREE-RANGE THOUGHTS

Ideally, you want to perform the above mentioned 'mental clean-up' on regular basis. This way you get into the habit of clearing your mind and also ensuring your great ideas and important to-dos don't get lost.

I use 'idea notebooks,' which I carry with me everywhere I go. It has been crucial to my ability to manage multiple projects at the same time and to fuel my creativity.

What you need is a handy, reliable tool that you can carry around at all times (maybe except the bathroom). It may be a good, old pen & paper solution, or the newest electronic gizmo.

Whatever you use, make sure this is a robust, reliable system:

- Use one system only, unless you absolutely have to use more. When I say 'a system,' I mean one way of recording in one place, be it pen & paper or an app. If you use multiple devices that automatically synchronise, that's okay too. But if you sometimes use a paper diary and sometimes an app on your phone, you increase the risk of your gems getting lost between the systems. Don't waste time transferring between systems and searching two systems for your recordings.

- You have it handy whenever you need it. Don't go for anything fancy or fiddly, or too big. At the end of the day, if you can't fit it into your smallest handbag, or it's something you'd be too self-conscious/embarrassed/scared to get out and use, you're not going to use it.

- It has to be something you can use with ease, as well, so if you're opting for a technology solution, make sure you're really familiar with it and that operating the app does not take longer than the recording of your thought.

- Always carry it with you; make sure it's charged (electronic), has room to record and all accessories required (your paper-based notebook is of little use without a pen/pencil).

- Use it, always; the moment a thought/idea worth capturing pops into your head, grab your device and record it.

- If you have a system in place, but somehow end up not using it as often as you should/could, something is not working. Review the system's usability and your own motivation to use it, tweak and try again; repeat until you always use it.

- Once you've written your entry, code it. Use something that is easy to understand for you, short, but informative enough to prompt you for what you need to do about/with this entry. You can use tags such as: to do, to follow up, blog post idea, etc. You can assign it to a category as well (work, holidays, family, university, etc.). Appropriate coding of your entries is particularly important if you're jugging several projects at the same time. Include important deadlines, and 'the next step' if this is the case.

- If your entry has a deadline, put it in your diary and schedule the necessary steps as soon as you can. Set up a system of prompting you to take action by using reminders and alerts (most time and task/project management apps/software will have that option, or simply use the diary on your phone).

There are many apps that can be used for this process. Evernote is probably the most known and most widely used. Do your research. You can also use the voice recorder/voice message option on your phone, or your e-calendar.

My 'idea notebooks' are real, paper-based small notebooks with a pen attached to it. I write one idea per page, or if I need more space, I staple the pages together as soon as I can. I fold one of the corners to 'tag' the entry by category (e.g., blog post, idea for a course). Upper corners are for creative ideas (blog posts, courses), bottom ones are for anything that's 'strategic' (e.g., steps in a marketing campaign). If the item requires any actions, I note it down. If there are any deadlines, I set a reminder on my phone: either with the deadline, or with a note to self to set up the timeline and deadline for this particular entry.

Test a few solutions before you settle for your favourite one.

STEP 3: BRING YOUR WANDERING MIND TO HERE AND NOW

The system described above is great for preventing your mind from wandering off. But what can you do if you actually find yourself distracted by your thoughts?

Here are two strategies:

- Identify, acknowledge, let it go

Identify you're distracted by [thought x]. Acknowledge it, by simply saying to yourself, 'I'm thinking about X (again).' And then, let go of it by saying to yourself something along the lines of, 'Oh, well. I need to focus on my task.'

- Snap out of it, with a gesture

You may want to use a physical or sensory action to help yourself 'snap out of it.' This technique is actually quite powerful and very effective, but it will take time and practice to work. The more you practice it, the better you get at it.

However silly it sounds, come up with your own little 'snap back into it' gesture. Physical (rather than just mental) actions work best because they enhance the signal you're giving yourself.

Some people put an elastic band on their wrist and lightly pinch/snap it. I touch my nose and say whatever my last word was aloud. Alternatively, I wave my hand as if trying to chase that though away. It took me a while to get these to work, but I've been using them successfully for several years now.

You can take a deep breath, or touch your nose, pat yourself on your wrists. Practice various little gestures until you come up with something that works for you as a reminder that you need to get back to your job.

BONUS: YES, YOU CAN MEDITATE, IF YOU LIKE

I need to disclose a conflict of interest here.

I don't meditate.

I'm not saying meditation is bad. I'm not arguing with the overwhelming evidence. Yes, motivation is the gold standard for stress reduction, improved cognitive skills, healthier body, happiness, and other great things, but it just doesn't work for me.

However, if you want a sharp focus, crystal-clear mind, bold decisions, supercharged memory, boosted creativity and many other physical and mental benefits—meditate. There is a plethora of resources available out there to help you learn to meditate. Check your local library, or consult a browser of your preference and enjoy.

MANAGING NEGATIVE SELF-TALK

Negative self-talk, telling yourself you can't do this, or that, or that 'You will never be able to…' or 'You're rubbish at…' is not 'just in your head. Evidence [3] shows that negative self-talk has detrimental effect on our performance. This is a well-known phenomenon in sport coaching [4], but not only in sports.

IF you don't believe you can do it, you have fewer chances at actually achieving your goal—it's the phenomenon known as self-fulfilling prophecy.

On the other hand, believing in your own abilities and chances of success increases your chances of the said success. [4]

There needs to be a balance here. Being overly optimistic about your own abilities and knowledge, particularly if the beliefs far exceed the actual level of skill/knowledge, is not good either. You have to put your work in, master the material, learn the skill, do the job—otherwise you're just deluding yourself.

But if you have put your hours in, done the job, and you still feel like you can't do it, you're 'never going to succeed,' or 'it's not good enough,' put a stop to your negative beliefs.

The crucial part is not to let it get from under your control, because negative self-talk can easily spill into a massive storm and completely take over your mind.

**Again, this is for information only, and should not replace professional advice from your healthcare provider. Check the resources section for references and further reading. If you have any difficulties managing your negative self-talk, thoughts and emotions, or suspect you may have a mental health problem, talk to your doctor. **

Here are a few strategies for getting negative self-talk under control:

IDENTIFY—ACKNOWLEDGE—LET IT GO

When you notice you're slipping into negative thinking again, pause and then identify the thought. Name what you're doing, e.g. 'I'm doubting myself again,' or 'I'm worrying it's not perfect,' and then, let it go, e.g., by imagining the thought disappearing into the distance.

ARGUE WITH IT

You can use the previously described strategy, but instead of 'letting go of it' (quite hard to perform at times), try arguing with the belief, e.g., 'Is that really true?' 'Is there another way of looking at it?' Use an example where you showed you can do it: 'Last week I did it quite well, actually.' Or use a positive counter statement: 'I have done this before, I know I can do it,' 'I have prepared for this presentation. I have all the skills I need.' etc.

I still get bouts of doubt and may slip into a negative self-talk at times of increased pressure, and this is my favourite technique for dealing with it. I usually go over the key skills/knowledge base needed for the task I'm about to embark on and prove to myself that I do indeed have those skills/have successfully completed similar jobs in the past.

TURN DOWN THE VOLUME AND LET IT FADE

This technique requires some visualisation, but can work quite well with a bit of practice. If you are a visual person, you can imagine the negative statement being written/printed in front of you. Now, let the colours fade and the font shrink. Keep going until you can barely see it.

If you prefer auditory metaphors, imagine you turn the volume down on the spoken words.

DISTRACT YOURSELF

Distraction is a simple technique that you can apply quickly in any situation. Although not as effective in the long run as the ones described above, it can still provide you with an 'exit trick' when you are unable to use any of the strategies described above and need a 'quick fix.' Try doing something that will completely absorb your mind: counting backwards/skip-counting backwards, solving a puzzle, or just singing a song you like.

One of my favourite tricks is to sing something, anything; often something that does not carry much meaning to me, but is 'sticky,' like nursery rhymes. It's a bit of an 'out of the frying pan, into the fire' strategy, because you may end up swapping the negative thought for a 'sticky song,' but (at least sometimes) a sticky but neutral song is better than negative self-talk.

Anthony Metivier, the creator of The Magnetic Memory Method, a memory palaces master, and a friend of mine, admits openly that conquering his negative beliefs was the first step to skyrocketing his ability to learn and memorise.

Even though he is the master of his memory and his mind now, he still has to deal with negative self-talk on regular basis.

Anthony's top tip for dealing with negative thoughts is to, first and foremost, not allow them to take over his mind and not get lost in that vicious cycle. 'I've learnt to live with them—be present with them every day.' He noticed that attending to basic needs, such as good nutrition and rest, can significantly lower the frequency and intensity of those thoughts. He also recommends regular meditation and exercise as great ways of preventing negative thoughts.

However, if he still catches himself slipping into negative thinking patterns, his favourite tricks for 'snapping out of it' is to visualise a volume knob on his thoughts and then turn it down. He also uses music, and for that he recommends music with positive lyrics—he picks a phrase, a positive statement, and keeps repeating it instead of the negative thought.

You can learn more about Anthony and his Magnetic Memory Method by visiting his website *Magnetic Memory Method* and listening to his podcast.

Well done, you've got to the end of this long chapter. By now, you know how to manage your emotions and use them for more powerful focus. You also have a range of strategies and tricks for keeping your mind on track and managing your free-range thoughts. In the next chapter, I will show you how you can identify and kill procrastination with laser-sharp precision.

PART 3 -

MOST COMMON

PROBLEMS AND HOW TO

DEAL WITH THEM

CHAPTER 8 - PROCRASTINATION: THE BULL'S EYE APPROACH

The third part of this book is dedicated to the most common focus problems and strategies for dealing with them.

This chapter is all about procrastination. We will be looking at:

- Recognising procrastination (it's not always what you think)
- The reasons people procrastinate
- Finding out why YOU procrastinate
- How to design your anti-procrastination campaign
- Targeted anti-procrastination strategies you can use
- Quick anti-procrastination tactics you can use

How many hours have you spent searching for the best procrastination tips & tricks? How many anti-procrastination apps have you downloaded? Have you tried 'motivation-boosting music,' Pomodoro, or even Internet-blocking software?

Has it helped?

Maybe a little?

Or a lot?

Not at all?

If you tried to deal with procrastination and are still struggling with it, stop searching for that silver bullet. There isn't any. They've lied to you. There are many great anti-procrastination tricks, but the key is that not all of them would work for everyone every time.

So what worked for your colleague, or the guy who wrote that hyped-up post you read yesterday, may not work for you.

Moreover, what helped you get stuff done last week may not work for you today.

Why?

Because there are many reasons people procrastinate, and even the same person may procrastinate over different tasks for different reasons, or for different reasons on different days.

The key to successful procrastination eradication is understanding why you're doing one thing when you should be doing another, and then choosing the right tool to deal with it.

To be honest, fighting procrastination is a war, not a battle. Even though you fix one thing today, it may still raise its ugly head tomorrow again. To win this war, you need to be prepared for a long haul and have an arsenal of weapons.

You need to understand why you procrastinate in a specific situation to choose a tool that would work for this particular context.

A master-procrastinator in one of my past lives, I've gathered a collection of weapons. I've tried and tested all of them. Some of them worked for some contexts, and some not. But I've learnt to recognise which approach is best for that scenario. I want to share my learnings with you.

Here is my bull's-eye approach to fighting procrastination.

How to recognise procrastination

The most common manifestation of procrastination is Web surfing or checking your social media accounts, and I'm sure you all can recognise that as procrastination. But what about some other, less obvious, or even sneaky activities you may engage in instead of focusing on the job you should be doing?

Here is a list of a few:

- Cleaning, organising, filing, etc.; organisational tasks, which in themselves are important to the overall productivity, but are not things that you should be doing NOW
- Working on low-priority tasks from your to-do list—just as with the example above, when you should be working on other things (see more about scheduling tasks according to your energy levels in Chapter 11).
- Attending to crisis after crisis and engaging into any other 'putting out fires' work; while these are all urgent tasks, they are not necessarily important jobs.

The key feature of procrastination is simply not doing what you are supposed to be doing at that time, even if you're doing stuff from your to-do list.

The main reasons people procrastinate:

Studies show that about 80% of college students and 15-20% of the workforce engage in procrastination on regular basis. [1]

Procrastination is a way of dealing with underlying, not always conscious, negative emotions such as fear, anxiety, or boredom. When you procrastinate, you avoid dealing with the unpleasant stuff and feel a little less unhappy. And if instead of your big scary job, you're working on low-priority items from your to-do list, you may feel productive, competent, and fulfilled.

The positive boost you get from procrastination never lasts long and is not powerful enough to fulfil you. The more you procrastinate, the more anxious and guilty you feel. Procrastination, by nature, results in loss of focus, progress, time and energy, quickly translating into failing to achieve your academic, professional, financial and even personal goals.

So why do people procrastinate?

The most common causes are:

- Fear of failure
- Fear of success
- Perfectionism
- Feeling overwhelmed by the task

- Feeling bored, uninterested, or otherwise unmotivated to do the task at hand or in relation to the bigger context (e.g., the entire project, your job, studies)
- Skill or knowledge gap
- Disorganisation
- Internal states (emotions, thoughts)

FIND OUT WHY YOU PROCRASTINATE

Above, I listed some common reasons people procrastinate. But in order to deal with your procrastination, you need to understand why YOU procrastinate.

I recommend you spend some time exploring the reasons behind you wasting your productive time on irrelevant or inessential activities.

The exercise I suggest is similar to the Distraction Log presented in Chapter 2.

Use a pen and a piece of paper, or any of your electronic tools. Go for something you're likely to use: easy to use, lightweight and handy.

Run the log for a few days and analyse the results.

You can use a template I prepared for you, which you can access on my website in the Bonuses Section http://www.theshapeshiftersclub.com/lsf-reader-bonus/—use "LSF reader" as the password.

You can also set up your own Procrastination Log. Don't forget to include: date & time, task you were supposed to be working on and activity you got engaged in instead.

The most important part of the log, however, is the WHY. Make the WHY column wide. You may need to spend some time exploring the underlying causes. It is time and effort-consuming, but it will be worth it. The better you understand WHY you do it, the better you will able to deal with it.

Just like with Distractions, keep asking yourself, "Why," until you arrive at what you believe may be the root cause.

Most commonly, you'll find your reason for procrastination in your relationship with the task you're trying to avoid. But if you're struggling to see that, look at the activity you've engaged in. What is it about this activity that makes you want to do this instead of the job you should be doing?

Use the list of the most common reasons for procrastination above as a guide.

Once you've got your results—analyse them.

Is there a pattern to your procrastination? Do you tend to procrastinate for a particular reason? Or on a particular type of task?

If you have a clear pattern (or more than one), you may want to use one of the strategies suggested below.

If you can't see a clear pattern, you may want to run those logs for a little longer to see if anything emerges. You can also just try some of the anti-procrastination tactics.

If you find yourself frequently working on tasks scheduled for another day/time, look into your energy and time management. See Chapter 11 for more tips on managing your energy.

HOW TO DESIGN YOUR TARGETED ANTI-PROCRASTINATION CAMPAIGN

Once you have a clear idea what your most common cause for procrastination is, design your own anti-procrastination campaign.

Below is a flowchart you can use as a guide to find your perfect anti-procrastination weapon.

Choose the best anti-procrastination tool for you:

Choose the best anti-procrastination tool for you:

1. I procrastinate often and (almost) always for the same reason:

Yes

No

2. I have time and motivation to implement a long-term solution

Yes

No

Develop a smart STRATEGY

Deploy a quick TACTIC

Choose your Ultimate Anti-Procrastination Weapon Fig. 1

3. Typically I procrastinate because:

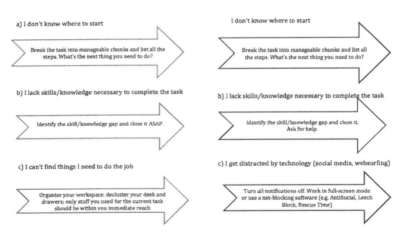

a) I don't know where to start

Break the task into manageable chunks and list all the steps. What's the next thing you need to do?

I don't know where to start

Break the task into manageable chunks and list all the steps. What's the next thing you need to do?

b) I lack skills/knowledge necessary to complete the task

Identify the skill/knowledge gap and close it ASAP.

b) I lack skills/knowledge necessary to complete the task

Identify the skill/knowledge gap and close it. Ask for help.

c) I can't find things I need to do the job

Organise your workspace: declutter your desk and drawers; only stuff you need for the current task should be within you immediate reach

c) I get distracted by technology (social media, websurfing)

Turn all notifications off. Work in full-screen mode or use a net-blocking software (e.g. AntiSocial, Leech Block, Rescue Time)

Choose your Ultimate Anti-Procrastination Weapon Fig. 2

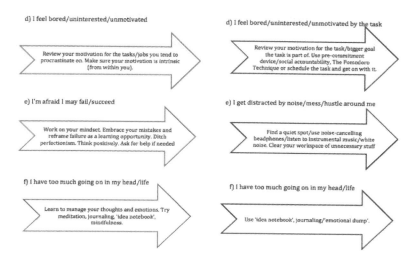

Choose your Ultimate Anti-Procrastination Weapon Fig. 3

For a downloadable version of this flowchart - check the Bonuses section of this book or go to my website, http://www.theshapeshiftersclub.com/lsf-reader-bonus/—use "LSF reader" as the password.

TARGETED ANTI-PROCRASTINATION STRATEGIES YOU CAN USE

Strategies are longer-term approaches that address the underlying cause. This is your ultimate procrastination weapon: very powerful and target-specific, but requiring time and effort to set up. A well-designed strategy will do the job every time, but only works for one procrastination cause. So if you procrastinate for a number of reasons, you will need a number of strategies to target the various root causes.

A strategic approach is best when:

- You have time and energy to develop and implement it
- There is a clear pattern to your procrastination
- You understand why you procrastinate or are willing to explore it
- You have tried tactics with limited success.

How to do it

Your Procrastination Logs will help you identify the underlying causes for your procrastination. Once you've got a clear idea why you procrastinate, whether it is a pattern, or just happens at times, use a targeted strategy to address it.

Below is a list of the most common procrastination causes, with a few suggested strategies to address them:

Fear of failure/fear of success/perfectionism

If you delay working on your task because you need more time to do research, learn more about it, find the perfect pictures/structure/topic, find the perfect pen, font, etc., or you're not sure what the right/best/ideal thing to say/do/write is, you're likely to suffer from perfectionism. Perfectionism is often driven by fear of failure.

It may be that you're feeling 'not good enough' to do the job, or don't want to make a fool of yourself in front of your boss, your friends, teachers, super fit guys in the gym... If this is your case, your biggest fear is failure, and failure to meet expectations—yours, your parents (even if you're a grown-up), your spouse, whoever else. These expectations are usually unrealistic, and usually in your head more than in the real world.

An interesting twist on this scenario is procrastination in the face of fear of success: 'What if I get it right and achieve my goal, and then people will think I'm a bore/cheat/self-centred/arrogant, etc.'

All three scenarios are typically driven by self-esteem issues, lack of confidence, anxiety over what other people may think/want from you. These are often issues deeper than what this book can deal with, so seek professional help if you need to.

Here are a few ideas on what you can do to help yourself overcome fear of failure, fear of success and perfectionism:

- Work on boosting your self-esteem and confidence
- Look at 'failure' as a learning experience. Remember Edison's quote? 'I have not failed 1,000 times. I have successfully discovered 1,000 ways NOT to make a light bulb.'
- Set yourself realistic goals and take smaller steps (check Chapter 3 for tips on how to do it).
- Stay positive and kind to yourself

A SKILL/KNOWLEDGE GAP

You delay working on your task because you are lacking knowledge or skill(s) required for completion of the task. This is a skill/knowledge gap scenario, well known to any beginners who have embarked on a project a little too far out of their comfort zone. If this is your favourite procrastination context, the best way to deal with it is to identify and close the gap. Investing time into exploring where your gap is and then learning what you need to learn pays off.

Look at where you struggle most or most often and ask yourself what it is that's getting in the way of you pushing on with your project.

Which part of your project is taking you a lot of time? Where do you get stuck? Where do you make most mistakes?

What do you think you need in order to move on with your project, or speed up the progress?

Usually, it's quite obvious, but if you're struggling to identify your knowledge/skill gaps, ask someone more advanced for help: teachers, tutors, senior colleagues, or even on a trustworthy online forum for enthusiasts.

FEELING OVERWHELMED BY THE TASK

You put off the job because it's too big and you don't know where to start. This is different from the scenario with the skill/knowledge gap described above. In this case, you do have the skills and knowledge required to get it done, but the task itself overwhelms you.

The best strategy for it is to break the task down into manageable chunks (see below for details). I must admit, this is the most common cause for my procrastination. That's why I've developed a system to deal with it.

1. Determine your goal.
What do you want to achieve? Do you need to finish your written assignment by Friday? Prepare a presentation? Whatever it is, make sure you understand where you want to get.

2. Break it down into elements/deliverables
What are the elements/deliverables of my overall goal; e.g., to prepare a presentation you need to:
- o Outline your presentation
- o Prepare the content
- o Make the slides
- o Practice the delivery

3. Plan how to get to those outcomes by creating discrete paths—one for every element/deliverable

4. Break down every path into clear steps
Always keep thinking: What is the next step? It is crucial that you are clear on what the next thing to do actually involves.

5. Prioritise those steps—decide what needs to get done first, second, third, etc.
This step may require some re-juggling and changing priorities as you discover that something needs to be done first in order for something else to get done, but that's fine. As long as you keep thinking about what needs to get done next and get it done, it should work okay.

6. Get on with it
You should have a work plan by now. Don't feel put off by its details. Yes, it may feel stupid to do so, but once you are so crystal clear about what you need to do next, it will be just a matter of working through your plan from the top down and crossing off those tasks.

Write it all down, so you don't have to remember and don't forget your steps. Check if you've got everything in, and... get on with it.

Feeling bored or under stimulated

If you find yourself not interested in the task at hand, or the whole project/study topic, or your profession in general, you are likely to procrastinate.

The same mechanism is involved in scenarios where you feel the task is too easy, not challenging enough, or you simply don't feel motivated to do that. The bottom line is lack of motivation for the task or the bigger context. Stuff you procrastinate with is obviously more interesting and/or more rewarding than the task you should be doing—no wonder your mind prefers to procrastinate.

Since this is a motivation/interest issue, you may need to review or boost your motivation. Check Chapter 4 for tips on improving your motivation.

Disorganisation

This is a common situation: your desk or office is too messy and you're forever looking for stuff, wasting valuable time and energy instead of getting jobs done. You may eventually decide to 'sort it out once and for all' and start a massive clean. As a result, your task does not get done. Having said that, organising and/or clearing your workspace is the right thing to do if disorganisation-driven procrastination is your case.

If your desk/workspace or office is messy, set aside time to organise it.

To prevent disorder impacting on your productivity and focus in the future:

- Learn to put things away where they belong
- Use a filing system
- Clean and clear your workspace regularly
- You can get inspired by The Toyota Way and its 5S: Sort, Straighten, Shine, Standardise and Sustain. This is a workplace organisation system famous for emphasising effectiveness and efficiency. The key principles as expressed by those 5S boil down to:
- Removing all unnecessary, not-in-use items

- Arranging items that are necessary and used to be easy to find and access
- Cleaning your workspace regularly
- Maintaining orderliness and standardising processes
- Regular audits, discipline and general keeping in working order

YOUR OWN THOUGHTS OR EMOTIONS

Struggling to turn off task-unrelated thoughts, or being distracted by your emotional state can also be a cause for procrastination.

The best way to deal with distracting thoughts and emotions is not to suppress them, but recognise, acknowledge and let go of them. So the next time your mind is buzzing with negative cognitions, such as 'I'm never going to learn it,' 'This is too hard,' 'I'm dumb,' or your emotions are getting in the way of your ability to focus, acknowledge/name them in a non-judgmental way, e.g.

'I'm doubting my abilities again,' or, 'I'm thinking anxious/stressed/ overwhelmed thoughts.'

and then—let go of the thought and move on. Keep repeating until the thought is gone—it takes practice, but it works in the end.

For more tips on dealing with thoughts and emotions, check Chapter 7.

QUICK ANTI-PROCRASTINATION TACTICS YOU CAN USE

If you're time poor and desperate for a quick fix to get that project report finished by a midnight deadline, pick one of many tactics.

Tactics are good because they are low-fuss. They don't require much up-front effort and you can make them work immediately. Some of them are context-specific, but most can be used for various situations. The downsides are that tactics don't address the underlying cause and hence may not work for you, or their effectiveness may be limited.

Be mindful, anti-procrastination tactics usually heavily depend on willpower, which can lead to willpower depletion, and that means it will not work for long. This is not an approach for habitual procrastinators.

Tactics are best when:

- You need a quick fix now
- You don't have a particular pattern to your procrastination
- It's a limited problem (and you are not a habitual procrastinator)
- You have strong willpower you can rely on

Tactic #1: Be target-specific

To successfully deploy a tactic, you need to target it at your specific procrastination behaviour. If the Internet is your poison, cut it off or limit your access with one of multiple apps/tools. If it's rearranging knickknacks/books/your collections of cars on your shelf, change rooms or sit with your back to the shelf to get away from the temptation. If it's playing a game on your tablet, lock your tablet in a drawer and put the key on the highest shelf you need a ladder for.

You get the gist—make it harder to access whatever is tempting you.

Tactic #2: Boost your motivation through peer pressure (a.k.a. social accountability)

Many of us are more likely to keep a promise we've made to someone who matters to us, than if we just 'sealed a deal' with ourselves.

Use the power of peer pressure and social accountability and tell people who matter to you—friends, family, your boss that you will do [that dreaded job/task] by [date], and ask them to hold you accountable. You can even ask them to nag until you've done it.

Another great strategy is to find an accountability buddy or group.

It is a risky tactic, though—there is a social price you pay if you don't deliver on your promise...

119

TACTIC #3: JUST GET ON WITH IT

This is the simplest and also the hardest approach: it's cold turkey, although you may want to sweeten the pill with some sort of reward for completing the task.

The secret of succeeding at it is... to just get on with your task.

Here are a few tricks:

- Do it first thing in the morning, or at night when you're not disturbed by anyone.
- Try the famous Pomodoro technique [2]: set a timer for 25 minutes ('Pomodoro') and work uninterrupted on your task. When the timer rings, take a short (3-5 min) break—have stretch, a drink, or just walk around (for more tips on effective breaks, check Chapter 6). You can take a longer break after 4 periods of 'Pomodoro.'
- Put your favourite (instrumental only) music on, or your favourite 'lucky' t-shirt.
- Schedule the task and turning up on the scheduled day & time, like you would do for an important appointment. And—get on with it.

Check Cal Newport's excellent post on his Fixed-Schedule Productivity. [3] You can read about it on his blog at http//calnewport.com (see Resources section for full link). He is selective in what he works on, and when. He keeps two streams of work projects (students and creative) to avoid the cost of switching between the streams. He also batches and turns his scheduled tasks into habits. It is a super-efficient and effective schedule that I still aspire to.

The best way of dealing with procrastination is to use a mix of approaches. I managed to get my procrastination under control by devising a strategy to deal with my most common cause (feeling overwhelmed by the size or complexity of the task) and using some tactical tricks (getting on with it with Pomodoro technique or scheduling) in the meantime, while working on getting into the habit of planning.

While I can't claim I'm completely procrastination-free, having an arsenal of weapons has catapulted me into much better productivity with less stress.

There is no easy trick, and it will take some effort, but once you've mastered a bunch of various techniques, and mixed & matched them with your situations, you'll be able to fight procrastination and get on with your job like a pro.

The bottom line is—be prepared for the war: pick a few weapons from the list and keep practicing. Test whether they work for you, and when. Try new things. Do anything.

Don't let Procrastination kill your goals.

Hopefully, now you have a clear understanding of why you tend to avoid doing what you should be doing. You also have an arsenal of weapons to target your procrastination. With that in mind, you can begin your war.

Or you can keep reading—in the next chapter, I'll show you how to tackle interruptions and distractions.

CHAPTER 9 -
HOW TO DEAL WITH
DISTRACTIONS AND INTERRUPTIONS

In this chapter I will give you some tips on dealing with interruptions and distractions.

While anything and anyone can be a source of distraction for you, typically distractions and interruptions come from:

- Your environment
- Your body
- Your mind
- And other people

I talked in detail about managing environment, body, and mind in Part 2, so here I will only touch on those issues.

For more information, see the corresponding chapter in Part 2.

1. DISTRACTING ENVIRONMENT (SEE CHAPTER 5 FOR MORE DETAILS AND TIPS)

The level of noise, type of lightning, ergonomics of your workstation, can all affect your ability to focus.

Scan your environment for potential distractors. The most common culprits include:

- Noise, particularly conversations, music with lyrics, ticking clocks
- Technology
- Uncomfortable chair/desk
- Light (too little or too bright)

Eliminate the distractors, if you can. If not, limit their effect on you.

NOISE

To minimise the effect of noise:
- Wear noise-cancelling earphones or earplugs,
- Use white noise or instrumental music to drown it out
- Avoid music with lyrics because lyrics, like conversations, tend to attract our attention. Our brains are wired to look for patterns and meaning. If you can hear someone talking or singing something, your brain will want to listen to it so it can make sense of it, in case there is some important information to pick up (such as the footsteps of a charging mammoth or a new place to find food). It's very hard to focus against the genetically-wired tendency, so avoid wasting your energy on it.

TECHNOLOGY

Technology is the biggest source of distractions these days, with all those buzzing, blinking, vibrating notifications your mobile phone, smartwatch, desktop, and any other electronic devices that are designed to attract your attention. Before you sit down to work or study, turn off anything that can make an unexpected sound, appearance or otherwise disrupt your focus.

WORKSPACE

Make sure your chair and desk are at the height comfortable for your height. If you're likely to spend a lot of time sitting at your desk, invest in a good, ergonomic chair. Think about the position of your wrists and your back. Consider getting a wrist-friendly keyboard and mousepad and a support for your lower back. It does not have to be expensive; something as simple as placing your laptop/keyboard at the right angle or using a rolled-up towel to prop your lower back can be enough.

LIGHTING

Inadequate lightning can turn your study or work session into a nightmare. Too dim or too-bright light will make you strain your eyes. Make sure there is no glare on your computer screen.

2. DISTRACTING BODY

Signals from your own body can be a source of distraction, too. Think of all those instances you couldn't focus on a lecture or a meeting because your chair was uncomfortable, you had a headache, were hungry, or needed a bathroom.

Having an ergonomically arranged workstation can help you avoid some of those pitfalls.

To keep your brain working at the top of its game, make sure you eat and drink adequately, too. It's not only what you eat and drink, but how you time your meals.

Tiredness and inadequate sleep significantly affect your ability to focus and maintain concentration. Make sure you get enough sleep and rest. Use breaks wisely.

For more information on managing these issues, check Chapter 6.

Manage your other physiological needs, address any aches and pains appropriately. If you have persistent or unexplained problems with your physical health, fitness, sleep, tiredness, etc., talk to your doctor or healthcare provider.

3. DISTRACTING MIND

Your mind is another source of distraction, and a powerful one, too. Unlike technology, it does not come with an 'off' button and cannot be exchanged for a more comfortable one, like a chair. But don't worry—you can learn to manage your distracting mind.

Here are a few tricks and techniques to help you minimise distraction and interruptions coming from your own head. For more, check Chapter 7.

CREATE A DISTRACTION-FREE ZONE

Organising your workspace in a way that supports and encourages you to sit there and focus on the task at hand will help you keep your mind on track. So, if you haven't done that yet, put it on your to-do list with high priority. Use tips offered above and in Chapter 5.

KEEP IT SHORT

Even when we try to deliberately focus on anything, our attention span is only 10 minutes, and then we tend to drift away, unless we try hard not to. With that in mind, plan your working/study sessions.

Obviously, taking a break every 10 minutes is inefficient and unrealistic. Schedule short, 5-10 minute breaks every 60-90 minutes. Use this time to get up, stretch, walk around, get a drink. Plan in longer breaks, too. For super-efficiency, use those 20-30 minute sections of time for meals, or your daily dose of exercise.

FOCUS ON ONE THING AT A TIME

Multitasking is a myth. People who multitask in fact task-switch and take twice as much time to complete tasks, making twice as many errors as those who concentrate on one thing at a time.

MAKE YOUR WORK/STUDY INTERESTING

Remember those times when you were so absorbed in your task, or play, you completely lost track of time? Positive emotions help us extend the attention span.

Start with the right, positive attitude even if you are struggling with the subject. Try to find something you like about it. You can also try to put yourself in a good mood before you sit down to study/work: talk to a friend, watch funny videos, listen to your favourite music (if it's before the session, it can be with lyrics).

Focus on meaning

Whether you are learning, writing, creating, or balancing the books, don't lose the sense of what the task means to you, why and how it's relevant to your overall goals. With a clear sense of purpose in mind, you are more likely to keep motivated and push on until it's finished.

4. Addressing distractions and interruptions caused by other people

We have talked about dealing with distractions coming from your environment, your body, and your mind. This was a warm-up to the next part—managing distractions caused by others. If you think dealing with yourself and things around you was hard, here is an even harder task for you. At least you have control or influence over yourself or your environment; it's not so easy and straightforward with other people.

Whether it's your colleagues, your friends, family, or even your flatmates, managing interpersonal relationships is usually more complex and delicate than simply rearranging your desk or turning your phone off. You cannot simply 'shut off' people who are close to you, because your actions may be perceived as rude and upsetting. Plus, more often than not, their support and help are invaluable and important to your success.

But if you spend so much time dealing with your nearest and dearest that it's affecting the quality of your work or your academic performance, you need to look at it honestly and consider what to do.

Here are a few tips on addressing distractions and interruptions caused by other people.

Don't work in a living/communal/public space

That's my husband's favourite line when I complain that I can't concentrate on what I'm doing while working on my laptop on the dining table.

If you want to focus on your task, don't work on it in a communal or living area. Communal areas, such as living and dining rooms, hallways, launderettes, shops, open office space, etc., are designed to facilitate human interaction, and there is usually a tacit agreement that whoever is there does not mind the noise and chatter, or being approached.

There are obviously some exceptions to it, such as libraries, reading/study rooms, churches/places of worship. But generally, you are more likely to be interrupted or distracted by other people and their coming and goings when you sit in a communal area..

IF YOU HAVE TO WORK IN A COMMUNAL AREA, CREATE A DISTRACTION-FREE OASIS

Sometimes we don't have a choice—be it because of limited space available, or because an open-plan office is what you get at work.

During my first year as a medical student I was boarding with a very nice lady who loved having her friends round for coffee once a week. Sadly, the walls in the apartment were very thin and I couldn't help but hear all the conversations and laughter. I didn't want to upset the otherwise super-nice landlady, so I started spending those afternoons poring over my textbooks at a local botanical garden. You may say 'out of the frying pan into the fire.' A botanical garden is a public space, but because it is an open space, where passing cars, people, dogs, and other sources of noise generally move around, the noise is easier to ignore. Even if there are people talking nearby, it may be easier to tune out and treat it as white noise.

To help myself 'tune out' and avoid distractions from passers-by (and crazily chirping birds), I was listening to classical music. It worked wonders (but only as long as the weather was good).

If well prepared, a public/communal space can be less distracting than your own home.

- Wear headphones, earplugs, etc. Whether you are listening to music (as explained before, I'd recommend instrumental over anything with lyrics), or just trying to block noise, wearing a set of head- or earphones, or earmuffs, not only will help you focus on your task, but will also deter anyone who may consider approaching you.

This technique can work well in an open-space office when you need to concentrate on your job without getting distracted by what your colleagues are doing.

Many of my fellow introverts use noise-cancelling headphones/earmuffs when traveling on planes, trains, and any other means of public transport where the person next to you may want to strike up a conversation. I must admit, I have used this technique successfully numerous times to avoid being dragged into a conversation I did not want to have.

Word of warning—obviously, by deterring people from approaching you, you may be risking not meeting or talking to someone interesting, or losing a potential or existing friend. Bear that in mind and make your choice according to your priorities.

- Use your environment to screen yourself off the rest of the room/world
  If you cannot bear sitting in an open space, use your environment to create a separation between you and the rest of the world.

  Books, papers, or magazines held right in front of the face, although uncomfortable after a while, can provide an excellent screen. The screen of your computer/laptop can play a similar role.

  If any of those things are not available, or not appropriate, find a spot where a piece of furniture can provide a separation. Potted plants, bookcases, open doors (be careful and mind the door) can work as screens.

  You can also sit with your back to the rest of the room, facing the wall.

- Put up a 'Do Not Disturb—Work in Progress' notice
  Our home office has a 'Work in Progress—Do Not Enter' notice with a piece of sticky tape by the door. If you want to concentrate on your work, stick it on and close the door. Otherwise, anyone can enter at any time.

  It took me a few conversations with my family, and particularly with my curious 6-year-old, but it works, at least most of the time. I definitely recommend explaining to your nearest and dearest (and flatmates) why you may need to put the notice on your door at times. Try to frame it in such a way that they can see what's in it for them (see below for tips).

I have worked in open-space offices and seen 'Do Not Disturb' notices on cubicle walls, people's desks, and even own backs (or chair backs). However ridiculous it may sound to you, these little pieces of paper do work. Most colleagues respected them, understanding this is the reality of a shared working space.

- Talk to people on your own terms

    The purpose of addressing distractions and interruptions caused by other people is to enable you to focus without damaging any relationships. This is why it's important that you communicate your intentions clearly to those around you. Be polite but assertive.

    o   Give them notice

    Telling your nearest and dearest that you are planning to work on your new book, math assignment, or board presentation and asking not to be disturbed for a period of time is a great way of minimising the risk of them walking in when you're in the middle of writing your next bestseller or brainstorming your essay.

    This can be as simple as informing your family, flatmates, or office mates that you are about to be unavailable for a (set a time) period of time and asking not to be disturbed. A brief explanation of the importance of the task and/or finishing the task on time may be helpful. As usual, the best arguments are those that show the impact of the job completed (or not) on the potential disturber/interrupter.

    In our house, adults respond well to deadlines that need to be met (because of reputation, other people relying on you, potential rewards from it), while children respond to something 'translated' into their world, e.g., money to be earned for holidays or to pay for their favourite activity.

    In an office situation, often jobs you need to focus on will have an office- or company-wide impact, even if only on a small scale. So tell them you need two hours to concentrate on finishing that data analysis so the rest of the team can progress to the next stage of the project.

    If your task does not have a direct impact on the potential disturber/interrupter, think of an indirect link. This may be as simple as, 'Hey, Joe! I'm going to clean the bathroom, just as we agreed, but absolutely have to finish the assignment today. I need a couple of hours only. Do you mind if I just concentrate on the assignment without any interruptions now and once it's done, I'll do the bathroom?'

o   Offer them your time beforehand

If you work with people who notoriously interrupt you with minor things, misjudge what's urgent, or simply pop in for a chat when you're trying to concentrate on your job, you may need another technique.

Obviously, if you want some peace and quiet to finish a report, you can just simply lock your door and disconnect your phone, if you have your own office, but this may not stop your colleagues from interrupting you. It may also be seen as rude and negatively impact on your relationships within your company.

Wherever interpersonal relationships are involved, whether you're the boss or a person at the bottom of the pecking order, respect others and tread carefully. Always balance potential gains from improved productivity with potential losses in relationships and office politics.

A while ago I had a work colleague who would come to my office to ask questions and 'pick my brains,' often multiple times per day. To make thing worse, she would only ask one thing at the time, so that it was 'really quick'. This was obviously quite disruptive to my workflow and it didn't take long for me to start brewing murderous ideas.

Fortunately, for her and my own future, I came up with another idea. Every time I was planning to work in peace and quiet for some time, I would pop into her office to check if she had anything for me. I would usually say something along the lines of, "Hi, Amy. I'm just about to lock myself in the office to prepare the [insert an important task of the day/week]. I won't be available for a couple of hours, so I'm just popping in to check if you have any burning questions or other issues I can help you with."

Initially, when I first started doing it, she would say that she did not have anything. Knowing her and wanting to avoid interruptions, I would stress, "It's now or never till tomorrow." I would do it with a light tone of voice and smile on my face, but also clearly indicating I would be locking myself in my office and not answering the phone or door.

It took us a couple of rounds with her furiously knocking on my door and calling out my name outside my office, and me sitting quietly at my desk until she walked away. I must say I felt a little guilty and weird the first time round, but persisted with my decision.

For the first few times, I would pop in to her office after I finished my jobs to ask if she had been looking for me earlier on. And then I would explain I had my headphones on, so couldn't hear her, and asked if she needed me for anything. She would usually blush and apologise for interrupting me. It wasn't anything urgent in the end. It took her one or two more incidences like that before she learnt, but overall it was worth it. A similar approach may work at home with your family or flatmates, too.

If you have a relative or a friend who tends to call you often, you can try phoning them before your work/study session to check in with them. Again, remind your nearest and dearest that you are about to retreat into your office/workspace for a period of time and will be uncontactable. Give them the reason why you want to do that now, and as always, try to present 'what's in it for them.'

If the people you want to use this strategy with need your support/help often, you can offer to check in with them after you have finished your work/study session, also. I found this approach works well with my child.

If you consider using this strategy, remember to weigh up pros and cons of this approach, how firm, gentle, or diplomatic you want to be, depending on what feels natural to you, but more importantly, on your relationships with your colleagues. I have chosen a quite straightforward approach, but soften it a little bit with a sense of humour and a little white lie for the sake of the relationship.

5. Don't let the 'energy vampires' leech on you

Jim Rohn, an American entrepreneur, speaker, and author said, 'You are the average of the five people you spend the most time with.' Yep, bad or good—they all influence who you are and shape your choices.

Are you happy with whoever you spend the most time with? Is there anyone in your world who makes you feel deflated, guilty, negative, irritated, anxious, overwhelmed, down or bored? Do you feel some people in your circle just drain you of your energy, vitality and will to live?

If you answered yes to any of those questions, you'll probably know what the term 'energy vampire' means. Psychologically speaking, these are people who are immature, self-centred, often emotionally incapable of giving and empathy.

Even if they don't take up too much of your time, the little moments spent with them leave you feeling like your life has been sucked out of you.

How do you manage an energy vampire getting in the way of your work?

There are a number of ways in which you can approach this issue. The actual strategy would depend, again, on your personal preference and interpersonal style (Does it sound like you? Can you do it or not?), your relationship with the 'vampire' (Is he/she your boss? Your mother? A distant relative? A colleague you don't work with often?), their effect on you (minor vs major, feeling bored/stressed/depressed), and other things.

- Keep your own emotional energy up by maintaining a positive support network, self-esteem, a sense of purpose and regular reflections on your feelings.
- Don't let them suck the life out of you when you are interacting with them. Remind yourself you have a choice of accepting or rejecting their point of view, or even arguing with it. Don't let their words and emotions take up space or linger in your head or your heart. Take a step back, creating a 'sanity buffer' and putting their words and action in perspective. Boost up your internal energy by self-affirmation and a clear sense of your purpose, values and worldview.
- Keep it light and short. If you don't have to interact with this person at a deeper level, keep your interactions focused on light topics. Change the topic tactfully when you feel it's drifted towards the dark, gloomy, unwanted content.
- Walk away if you can.
  What's your motivation for having this person in your life at this stage? What's the price you're paying for it? Is it worth it?

If the cost/benefit ratio of this relationship is negative, consider walking away from the relationship, or putting firm boundaries/limits on any interactions. You may want to think of less impactful ways of communicating, e.g. emails instead of face-to-face meetings or phone calls or time-limited calls. Try being as much in control of those interactions as you can, e g. you call the person instead of the person calling you.

DEALING WITH FRIENDS WHO BECOME ENERGY VAMPIRES AT TIMES

And then, there are people who are generally good and lovely, and can be great friends, but in certain circumstances can easily change into energy vampires.

I had a good friend at uni, an absolute treasure of a person. But before exams she would turn into a super-anxious perfectionist. Any conversation with her would be filled in with worst-case scenarios, the most difficult questions ever asked, obscure facts dug up from old textbooks and the like. All that was sprinkled with panic—there is so much to do and so little time left and the professor is in bad mood.

Every time I spoke to her in the exam prep context, I would get caught in that mood and struggle to shake it off. So I decided to put some boundaries around my contacts with her during exam time.

If we talked, I would listen to her for a while, but not let myself get sucked into the panic. I would ask her to change the subject at some point, explaining that I'd rather talk about something that would take my mind OFF the exam. She was okay with that.

I also developed an alternative 'point of reference' system specifically for exams and other assignments. I had a group of 2-3 friends with whom I would discuss exam-related stuff in more detail, because their approach to exams helped me keep my own anxieties and worries under control.

I am a big fan of being honest and respectful with your friends, so I would normally have a respectfully honest conversation with my friends. I was also lucky enough to have friends with similar attitudes to these things. I realise not everyone is able to do that, and it may not be possible to do with everyone. You need to exercise your judgement in how you are going to approach those conversations. Sometimes diplomatic silence or a white lie is the best option.

This chapter focused on dealing with interruptions and distractions, including the delicate matters of dealing with people who interrupt and distract us. In the next chapter, I will address the growing problem of shrinking attention span.

CHAPTER 10 -
PROBLEM WITH ATTENTION SPAN?
NO PROBLEM!

Let me stress it from the beginning: this chapter is not about ADHD/ADD (Attention Deficit Hyperactivity Disorder/Attention Deficit Disorder). If you suspect you may have symptoms of ADD/ADHD or any other mental or physical disorder which is affecting your attention span, seek professional help.

But if you're otherwise healthy and yet struggling to keep your focus on one thing for periods long enough to achieve anything, keep reading. I will be addressing:

- The modern world's Short Attention Span Curse
- The reality of attention span
- And how to improve your attention span

In the modern world of pressure to do more, faster and while being always online, our ability to focus on one task at a time diminishes. I have met many adults who felt their attention span have shrunk later on in life, even though they never had attention problems as kids.

They are waking up already in a hurry, multitasking to the point of trying to use their toothbrush to comb their hair, replying to emails while eating breakfast and watching the news at the same time.

Impatient, bored, restless, dissatisfied, with a tendency to go for multiple, simultaneous and superficial rather than mono-focus and in depth, we blame modern technology, TV and/or the advertising industry for our problems.

Maybe the technology is to blame. Or maybe not—it's not for me to judge (there are studies proving the point and studies proving the opposite—see the end of the chapter for references). But many of you would probably agree with me—it is harder to keep your mind focused on one thing for longer these days than 20-30 years ago.

ATTENTION SPAN—THE REALITY

If you've read Chapter 1, you may remember how our attention works, but if you haven't, here is a brief outline.

In a nutshell, we have two types of attention: **automatic and intentional**.

Automatic attention's job is to alert us to any changes in our environment, so that we can save our lives. It is designed to grab us by any means. It is triggered by unexpected sounds, flashes of light, pain pangs. It lasts only a few seconds, but because of the way it's geared up, it can destroy your focus for a while. Think: ambulance sirens, lightning, that shooting pain in your neck when you turn your head too quickly, but also phone ringtones, pop-up email notifications, and toasts jumping out of the toaster. They are hard to ignore, and are best avoided.

Intentional attention is that part of our ability to focus that is in our control. It's the 'I want to watch that video right now,' or 'I am listening/reading/talking to you in this very moment.' Notice the element of conscious choice and intention to be engaged in the activity. However, by itself, intentional attention will only last 10 minutes. If you don't fuel it with genuine interest, it will drift away to the next interesting thing.

As you can see, attention by itself does not last long. That's sad news, but it's not all bad news. Obviously, since we can manipulate our attention, we can also influence its span. Once you know how it works, it's easy to figure out how to extend its span. It is not rocket science, but requires some time and a lot of practice.

I admit, I feel I am a victim of this modern 'attention-shortening' disease. I have fallen asleep during lectures and meetings, walked out of boring films and dumped books because the plot was developing too slowly for my liking. I have not to date achieved my dream of running a half-marathon, because runs longer than an hour bore me out of my skull, and so does listening to anything longer than 20 minutes.

You may remember that my most common reason for procrastinating is long-term, complex jobs.

Yes, I am a short distance runner, but after many years of agonising over fat textbooks and snoring during lectures, I have developed a few strategies to extend my attention span.

The strategies for extending short attention span fall into one of two buckets:

1. Minimise the impact of Automatic Attention, which boils down to minimising distractions
2. Maximise Intentional Attention, which is about extending your ability to focus beyond those natural 10 minutes.

Let's now look at these two main strategies:

1. Minimise distractions

Automatic attention has a powerful effect on us because it is ultimately a survival strategy. That's why it is so important to address this aspect of your short attention span first.

How?

This will be nothing new to you, because we've covered it earlier in the book, but let me quickly reiterate it:

- Make your environment a distraction-free zone:
- Manage technology: turn off notifications, your phone, messenger, emails
- Scan your workspace for any potential sources of unexpected sounds, visual signals, etc., and eliminate if you can. If not, manage it (e.g., wear

noise-cancelling earmuffs, put on white noise, throw away that flickering lamp. For more details, check Chapter 5.).

- Look after your body: make sure you get enough sleep, exercise, food and fluids, don't forget about bathroom breaks and schedule breaks into your work/study plan. Seek medical/health professional help if needed. (For more tips on looking after your body for a better focus, check Chapter 6.)

- Manage your mind: your mind-set, your emotions, your thoughts, etc. (Check Chapter 7 for more details.)

- Address any interruptions or distractions caused by other people. (you will find more about it in Chapter 9.)

- Keep it short: be aware of the fact that unless you're interested in the task/job, your attention may drift away after 10 minutes. Boost your motivation for longer and more complex projects (see Chapter 4 for tips) and plan shorter and longer breaks (see Chapter 6 for tips).

MULTITASKING—A SPECIAL MENTION

Attention is like a filter that limits the amount of information that enters and remains in our memory. It's our ability to concentrate on a task without becoming distracted. Please note, I am talking here about A task—one task. Why?

Because our brain is able to consciously concentrate/focus attention only at one task at a time. Multitasking is a myth.

Of course, our brain is running several applications simultaneously, such as breathing, blinking, making our heart beat, coordinating complex muscle movements and many, many more. But these actions do not require conscious attention or awareness and are not recorded in memory.

For those things that need our awareness, interest and memory to be at work, we can only focus on one task at a time. Multitasking is actually a task and attention shifting exercise. Multiple studies show that people who play the 'multitasking game' take twice as long to complete a task and make 50% more errors than those who don't. [1, 2] So if you want to improve your focus and get your job done faster, with fewer errors, stop multitasking now.

2. MAXIMISE YOUR ATTENTION SPAN

Another way to improve your ability to focus for longer periods of time is to work on extending your Intentional Attention. Let's look now at some ways of doing it.

Do you remember when you last got so lost in a task you forgot all about the time? Maybe you were playing your favourite game, or exploring a really interesting topic? Or maybe you were engaged in your hobby, or something at work?

How did you feel?

Energised? Totally focused? In control? Learning effortlessly? Happy to the point of ecstatic?

If yes, chances are you were 'in the zone,' or to use a more formal term, experiencing Flow.

Flow is the state of 'focus on steroids' and a 'Holy Grail' of high-performance seekers.

You may remember from Chapter 3 that Flow happens when we are working on something that challenges us and demands a high level of skill, but we feel we have what it takes to get it done. Here is a simple graph (again) to illustrate our reactions to various levels of skill and challenge:

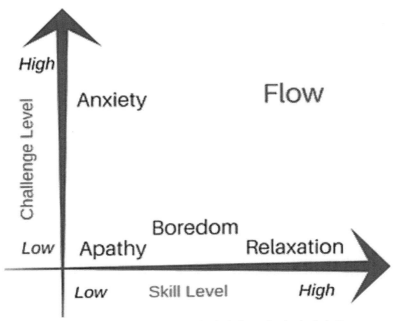

Model of Flow as a function of the level of skill vs the level of challenges as per Csíkszentmihályi [4]

According to Owen Schaffer [3], an expert in user research and a student of Mihály Csíkszentmihályi (the Flow pioneer) [4], the conditions for creating flow are as follows:

- Knowing what to do
- Knowing how to do it
- Knowing where to go (if there is navigation)
- High perceived challenges
- High perceived skills (yours)
- Freedom from distraction
- And feedback

Based on that, we can put together a recipe for 'never-ending' attentions span:

- Get rid of distractions
- Have a level of knowledge and skills that enables you to do the task
- Have a clear plan/goal for the task

- Make sure your task-at-hand still requires you to learn and/or challenges your skills/knowledge
- Seek immediate feedback

There is also another key ingredient—a genuine interest, intrinsic motivation for approaching the task.

And if you go back to your memories of being 'in the zone,' you will remember this was when you were doing something you deeply cared about, had a passion for or simply enjoyed.

Positive emotions enhance our ability to focus on a task at hand, and you can use them to improve your attention span.

The best way to extend your attention span is to ensure you are actually interested in the task at hand. However, this may sometimes not be the case. Young people, students in particular, face this challenge quite often.

I get asked this question a lot: "But what if I don't like/I'm not interested in my subject? I am only studying this [insert study subject/topic/job] because my parents made me do it/it pays well/it's popular/easy [insert an extrinsic motivation of your choice]."

If you are not motivated to work on the task, or if your motivation is only external and the task requires time and effort, it is likely you will struggle to focus for prolonged periods of time. Or even for more than those 10 minutes.

How to address lack of interest/motivation for the task/job at hand

1. Sort out your motivation/intrinsic motivation
   If you're lacking intrinsic motivation for the job/task you need to focus on, I suggest you review it. Check Chapter 4 for tips on how to do it.

2. Add emotions
   If you read Chapter 7, you will know how emotions affect our attention. If you haven't, you can go back and read it. Here is a brief summary: Emotions attract our attention. We pay attention to anything that's emotional, negatively or positively: joy, happiness, or fear, anger.

Emotions, positive or negative, can hold sway over our ability to focus, think, process information and concentrate.

With their promise of a 'mental and physiological high,' emotions provide an attractive and powerful distraction, which is very hard to resist if the task is mundane, boring and dry.

In Chapter 7, I explained how these properties can impact negatively on your focus. But there is a positive side to it, too.

Since we pay attention to anything that is emotional, emotions can enhance our ability to be attentive and remember. The trick is to find that sweet spot where your emotional state enhances rather than hinders your ability to focus.

Adding emotions to whatever task you're trying to concentrate on will help you keep your focus on it for longer. Interestingly, research shows it doesn't really matter if we use positive or negative emotions. Both modalities can enhance your ability to concentrate on the task at hand and perform. Apparently, positive emotions, such as joy and happiness, help us think creatively and problem-solve, while anxiety or anger are more likely to enhance our analytical thinking and attention to details. [5]

It takes some trial and error and exploring to find your optimal spot. Be mindful not to 'overdo' negative emotions, because too much of that stuff is more likely to affect your focus negatively.

Here are a few ways in which you can enhance your focus with emotions:

- Set up your environment to enhance your preferred emotional state:
- Use your favourite colours, favourite props, tools, smells, etc., to enhance the sense of joy, happiness.
- Create a sense of stress or time pressure by reminding yourself of a tight deadline or setting up one yourself—a countdown clock/timer or calendar with the due date circled in red can work very well. Deadlines, even self-imposed ones, can be a very effective way to enhance your focus.
- Do something that makes you laugh or smile before your session. Listening to your favourite happy music is the most common way of 'inducing' the sense of joy and positive energy (listening to songs with

lyrics prior to the session is okay, it's during the working/study session when lyrics become more of a hindrance than help to focus).

For some people it is talking to someone they like/love. For others, playing with their pet.

And, yes, you can watch those funny videos on YouTube, or LOL Cats—just don't turn it into a procrastination session.

- Do something that makes you feel accomplished, successful, even if it is washing a pile of dishes.

   I had a friend who claimed that cleaning helped her learn—she would clean her study room and neatly arrange all her gear on her desk and bookshelves before her every studying session. She said it gave a sense of pride and calm: that everything was orderly and under her control.

- Chat to someone you like/love

- You can also dip your toe into the negative emotions, but be careful. I've already mentioned using deadlines and time-pressure related stress. I know that some people are motivated by a fear of failure or anger. Try it, if it's your cup of tea, but be careful not to overdo it.

3. HAVE AN ACCOUNTABILITY/BUDDY SYSTEM

Pairing up with a colleague, friend, or a fellow student can boost your ability to extend your attention span, too. This way you create a sense of obligation you would want to fulfil, which will add fuel to the fire under your tail, and will keep you working on that project, or tasks, or whatever it may be for longer.

4. HAVE A REWARD SYSTEM

Go on, use a promise of that chocolate bar, your favourite procrastination activity, or some other trick to reward yourself for completing the task. But please, bear in mind that too many extrinsic rewards can kill your internal drive to do the job, so be careful not to overdo it.

The best way to reward yourself is through whatever connects to your sense of pride, achievement, of hope for the better future—all of which may and could be linked to whatever you're doing. For more tips on engaging your intrinsic motivation, check Chapter 4.

5. HAVE A PLAN

Start where you are now and gradually extend the amount of time you spend focused on your task.

- A good rule of thumb is to increase it by 10%, but start small so that you can say no and you can only succeed. If you're starting from a 10-minute period of time, it means only 1 minute longer.
- Set a timer and sit at your desk/workbench until the sound beeps. Initially, you may struggle to concentrate on the task, but keep going, even if you're able to focus only partially, or going 'in and out.' In the worst-case scenario, just sit there, staring at the table/computer/textbook, but try to refrain from doing anything else.

Keep at it until it becomes more comfortable.

If you've successfully completed the first challenge, you can try extending the period of focusing on your task the next time, and build from there.

If you really struggled to stay on task the first time around, continue at the same level until it becomes less arduous. You can also half the increase, e.g., if you extended your period of focus by 1 minute, try extending it by 30 seconds only, and increase only once this is comfortable.

6. INCLUDE BREAKS

Your plan should include breaks. Ideally, your shorter (3-5 minutes) breaks should be every 60-90 minutes, and longer every 2-3 hours.

However, if you're not able to sit and concentrate for 60 minutes, you may need to take a short break after every period of focus, however short it is, and reserve longer breaks for meals, etc.

When I first started, I had to take many frequent breaks. Often this would be just to get up and stretch, or walk around the flat. I would try to make it as short as possible and I would then drag myself back to the desk. Gradually, I managed to extend the periods of sustained focus to a decent 50-60 minutes. Now, I can easily sit and type away for longer than that, but usually need to get up and move around after about 60 minutes to look after my back.

Check Chapter 6 for more tips on effective breaks.

7. KEEP PRACTICING

Extending your shrunken attention span will take some time. Don't worry if you can't immediately focus for those 'ideal' 90 minutes. Look at ways of adding emotions or rekindling your intrinsic motivation for the job, or the bigger picture. Keep working on it gradually, and you will notice a difference soon.

In the next chapter I will dive into the problem of managing time, and explain why managing energy is a better way to improve productivity and ensure your focus is always best for the task at hand.

CHAPTER 11 -
THE IMPORTANCE OF
MANAGING ENERGY, NOT TIME

In this chapter I want to tell you about another productivity myth—the myth of time management and the magic of energy management. I will show how to ensure your energetic resources don't dry up and how to factor your energy management into your day.

If you have ever struggled to get jobs done even though you have fantastic motivation, the best productivity tools, and top-notch time-management skills, you'll know what I'm talking about.

Many people believe that time is the most precious resource we have.

Wrong.

I have heard productivity gurus say, "Time is a non-renewable resource: once it's gone it's gone forever."

Again, wrong.

Even though, once this morning is gone, it's gone forever, you still have some of today left, and tomorrow is another day (assuming you wake up). All you need to do is to get out of bed.

Yes, time is a finite resource and we should therefore use it wisely. But on the other hand, time is actually a renewable resource.

However, if you are tired, sick or feeling mentally exhausted, no matter how much time you have left today, you're not likely to make much happen.

With all the time in the world and mountains of motivation, but no physical, mental, emotional or spiritual energy, will your jobs get done?

I doubt it.

This is why we should be really managing our energy, not our time.

I've learnt it the hard way. Only about a year ago I was still squeezing tasks, meetings and calls into every available minute of my day, saying yes all those potentially fantastic opportunities and then cutting back on sleep to find time to get it all done.

Yes, I had accomplished a lot in a short period of time.

But then, things started to crumble down. I began to feel exhausted, washed-out, my creativity dwindled and I started feeling quite disengaged.
It took me several months to get back on track. It was painful. I had to rethink not just my priorities, but also my principles. Getting more done in less time with a 'zero waste policy' had to be replaced with more down-time and a much slower pace. And although I am doing much better now, I'm still not fully recovered.

I don't want you to make the same mistakes. Don't let the productivity drive mislead you away from the real productivity. The key to sustained top performance is not a bursting-at-the-seams diary and always working 'full steam ahead.'

If you want to always work at the top of your game, start managing your energy.

THE SECRET TO LASTING FOCUS

What's energy?

According to the Merriam-Webster online dictionary, [1] energy is the ability to be active: the physical and mental strength that allows you to do things. It is also 'natural enthusiasm and effort,' and 'usable power that comes from heat, electricity, etc.'

All those definitions relate to physical and/or mental energy.

Physically and physiologically speaking, energy (for humans) comes from food and hydration and is restored by sleep and rest. We talked about optimising your body for maximum mental effort in Chapter 6.

But physical energy is not enough for focus.

Mental strength comes from a clear mind and healthy emotions, which we covered in Chapter 7.

Is that all?

Not quite.

For the complex beings we are, ensuring a steady supply of physical or mental energy is not all. To be active, full of 'natural enthusiasm,' and capable of effort, we need more than food, rest and a clear mind.

Tony Schwartz and other creators of The Energy Project advocate for a different view of human energy. According to their research, nearly 60% of workers are 'physically depleted, emotionally drained, mentally distracted, and lacking in meaning and purpose.' [2] Schwartz and his colleagues distinguish 4 types of energy—all of them essential to our work-life balance and overall wellbeing:

- Physical energy is about your physical health, your ability to move your body at the required speed, in the required direction. The biggest influencers of your physical energy are sleep and nutrition.
  We covered that in Chapter 6.

- Mental energy is about your ability to focus on the job at hand, manage distractions, procrastination, decision-making and willpower battles. It is also your ability to do bigger-picture work: strategizing, goal-setting, planning and reflection.
  We covered these topics in Chapter 7.

- Emotional energy refers to your emotions, and happiness in particular. Research shows that positive emotions boost productivity by as much as 12%, while unhappy people are 10% less productive than an average person [3].

You can find tips on how to harness your emotions to improve your focus in Chapter 7 as well.

- Spiritual energy is a little more complex and refers to doing what really matters to you, maintaining integrity, being driven by a sense of purpose and autonomy. I hinted at these aspects when I explained how motivation works and how intrinsic motivation is the driver of your long-distance projects (Chapter 4).

All these four types of energy are essential to fully engaged functioning in our daily life.

Yes, in order to be able to focus effectively for long periods of time, we need to make sure our physical, mental, emotional and spiritual energy supplies are alive.

How do you do that?

How to Ensure Your Energy Sources Don't Dry Up

In his article 'Relax! You'll be more productive,' Tony Schwartz [4] presents multiple studies that prove how taking time to renew energy boosts performance.

Sleep deprivation kills our ability to learn and recall—we already know that (Chapter 6). A good night's sleep boosts performance, and so do naps [5]. Quality leisure time and holidays are linked with better physical and mental health, ability to cope with stress and demands of work. [6] Moreover, emotional wellbeing increases our productivity, too. Happy people are 12% more productive. [3]

I often see questions: How can I work/study for (12+) hrs. a day without burning out? Is it possible to work 100-hour weeks? My answer is yes, it is possible and I have 'been there, done that.' The question is not 'is it possible,' but, 'how long are you able to sustain it and what are you willing to sacrifice?'

When you're a junior doctor/doctor in training, you not only have to work long hours, you are EXPECTED to do so. Normal ward work, then on-call duties, whole weekends spent at hospital. Well, there is even a little competition about who can work longer hours... I'm guilty of doing that, too. At some point, I was doing 50-55 hour working marathons, because I also had an evening job as a language tutor. Yay!

But I was young and passionate about everything I was doing at the time. I did not have a family and I thought I was invincible. I also needed the money very badly.

I was able to sustain it for a couple of months and then I crashed.

I'm sure many of you have similar experiences.

Everything in life comes with a price tag. Although you may be able to pull off all-nighters and long working weeks, once every so often or for periods of time, this is unsustainable long-term. Our bodies and our minds are just not able to take it.

Physical, emotional, mental and spiritual energy are crucial to fully engaged functioning at work and in life.

But how can you ensure your 'energy sources' don't dry up?

Energy renewal is key to effective energy management and further productivity and effectiveness. If you want to be able to function at the top of your game, you need to allow or even facilitate the renewal.

I. Cover the Basics

First things first: make sure you sleep enough, eat well, hydrate your body and your brain. Don't abuse substances. (Check Chapter 6 for more details about keeping your body at the optimal performance level.)

2. Schedule Time for Renewal and Recuperation

I know, we're all busy. And sometimes we think we're so busy we can't afford a break. Yep, this is what I thought until over a year ago, when my body forced me to take a break. I got to the point where I would walk through the door after work with only enough energy to get myself to the sofa and fall asleep.

I was mostly exhausted mentally and emotionally, but my physical energy levels were pretty down, too. So I had to slow down. I had to slow my pace of work, take 2-3 week-long 'mini-holidays' between my projects, and schedule breaks into my diary.

Believe me, you CAN afford taking time for rest and restoration. Moreover, you CANNOT NOT afford it.

- Schedule breaks into your diary: shorter—more often, longer—every couple of hours. Shorter breaks can be as short as just walking around the building or going up and down the stairs. Take time to eat lunch when it's lunch time, and unless you absolutely have to take calls, put your phone on silent or leave it on your desk.
- Holidays and vacations can be good for recharging—make the most of the time off you can get. If you're working for yourself (like me now), make sure you have time put aside for holidays. Calculate how much you need to work to cover your needs and try to resist doing 'a little bit more' once you've reached your goals and you have a little more 'down time.'
- Disengage from work after work and on holidays, turn off your phone, don't check your emails if you are able to (I'm aware this is not always the case and some people may be expected to be contactable even during holidays/time off). Meet up with friends and don't talk shop.

3. LOOK AFTER YOUR EMOTIONS

Your emotional energy is replenished when you engage in activities that bring you happiness. So spend time with people you love and who love you—your friends and family. Do things you love doing. Do things you're good at and strive to grow.

Do things for others. Don't forget to count your blessings and appreciate what you have—it's proven to increase your sense of happiness. Start a gratitude journal and express your appreciation towards others.

These are all scientifically proven ways of increasing happiness. [7]

Do all of it, or at least some, on regular basis even if initially it feels artificial and awkward. At some point it will start flowing more naturally and you will notice a difference.

I have.

4. DON'T BE AFRAID TO DAYDREAM AND REFLECT

Yes, in Chapter 7 I gave you tips on harnessing your wandering mind. But while a wandering mind is not good when you're trying to focus on a job, it is not all bad news.

There is a scientific evidence linking daydreaming with creativity. [8] Creativity is not only the ability to write, compose music, or come up with Nobel Prize-winning ideas. It is also about ability to solve tough problems, be innovate, and just simply appreciate the beauty of the world around you.

Allow yourself time for reflection, reading poetry, and letting your mind loose.

5. ATTEND TO YOUR SPIRITUAL NEEDS

Daydreaming time is also time for reflection and reconnecting with the bigger forces in your life, whatever you call them. Reflection time also provides you with opportunity to refresh your sense of purpose, finding meaning, reconnect with the greater forces, whatever you want to call them. It is time to refuel your spiritual energy.

Your spiritual energy level will depend on your ability to be faithful to your values and principles, a sense of control over your destiny and decisions, having a 'noble goal'—a clear sense of purpose that you are able to pursue.

6. Schedule some procrastination

Yes, you've heard me right. In today's super-productive world where our value is measured by the goals achieved, it is hard to allow yourself to engage in seemingly aimless activity. But don't feel guilty about stuff you do that doesn't have a clear goal, such as playing your favourite game, flicking through a book, or just browsing the Net. Although if you're doing it when you should be doing something else, it is procrastination, this is not always the case.

Scheduled/structured procrastination is becoming more and more popular, particularly among creative types and anyone who needs to keep their creative juices going. Because, as I said above, if you let your mind wander off, you're boosting your ability to solve problems, innovate and grow as a person.

If you want to 'bump it up a level' and unleash some proper creative energy, go for a walk, lie on the floor with your eyes closed listening to music, exercise, or go out for lunch. Whatever you do, don't see it as being lazy, or wasting your time. These activities are important for energy renewal and creativity, so just embrace it.

7. Respect your natural rhythms

In Chapter 6 we talked about ultradian rhythms: those 60-90-minute-long bursts of activity interspersed with periods of rest. If you're able to work in periods of activity this long, go ahead—make the most of it. However, if you need breaks more often, arrange a schedule that suits your needs.

Use the principles presented in Chapter 6 to ensure your breaks are optimal.

If you're looking for a more refined work schedule, consider exploring your natural energy flows and aligning the type of work you do with them.

Analyse your natural rhythms in respect to the different types of energy and find out what your patterns are. This exercise will allow you to discover when you're at your best physically, mentally and emotionally. In my experience and understanding, spiritual energy does not really fluctuate during the day and it is more stable over time. However, it can drop and lead to burn out if not attended to. Once you've got a clearer picture of how your energy peaks and drops throughout the day, you can align the tasks you have to do to fit in with your energy states at the time.

I covered this topic extensively in my blog post: 'How To Achieve Top-Notch Productivity Without Having To Ditch Your Favourite Procrastination Habit,' which you can find in the Bonus Section on my website: http://www.theshapeshiftersclub.com/lsf-reader-bonus/—use "LSF reader" as the password.

8. Don't Mistake One Type of Energy for Another

Recognising where the deficiency or need is can be tricky at times. Boredom can mask as tiredness. Working in an environment where you compromise your values all the time is likely to bring on negative emotions, mental drain and even physical health problems. It pays to spend time to identify where the problem is so that the solution you apply addresses the underlying need.

I'm guilty of refuelling my physical energy bucket (with food and sleep), when I'm bored and unmotivated (mental energy), or even emotionally drained.

Observe yourself and ask yourself 'what's going on for me now?' as many times as you need to get to what's underneath it.

9. Start with First Things First

It's hard talking or thinking about working in line with your values if you're feeling tired all the time, or never have time to make and review your long-term goals. Maslow's hierarchy of needs is hard to ignore—you have to make sure you have your food and shelter safe and secure before you focus on following your passion.

Find out what is the most important of your energetic needs (and this varies over time and depends on your current context) and attend to those needs first.

For me, and probably for many of you, the physical energy comes first—it's really hard engaging into even the most enjoyable activity when you're falling asleep, or getting dizzy because of low glucose levels in your body.

Still feeling tired, irritated or empty? Put away your diary and stop looking at the clock. Don't flog that exhausted horse, it will not get you there today, no matter how hard you try.

So stop trying.

Look at how your physical, mental, emotional and spiritual powers are doing and make sure their sources don't dry up.

You know how to do it now.

Stop managing time and start managing your energy. This is a long-term strategy for always working at the top of your game.

In the next chapter, I will explain how stress affects your focus and your overall cognitive powers, and what to do to get on top of that.

CHAPTER 12 -
STRESS AND FOCUS:
THE GOOD, THE BAD, AND THE UGLY

In this chapter I will explore how stress affects our ability to focus. I will talk specifically about stress that can boost our cognitive powers, the type of stress that kills our brain and how to manage stress for better focus.

Stress is part of our everyday life. You can't escape, and why would you? It is also the spice of life. Stress motivates us to get better, run faster and... well, survive. If it wasn't for our internal stress management system, humans would have become extinct thousands of years ago.

But how does stress affect our ability to focus and perform mental tasks?

It depends.

First of all, stress is subjective—not everyone finds the same things stressful. However, there are a number of life events that most people would find stressful, such as the death of a close person, a serious illness, significant financial difficulties, or happy events like weddings, children being born, etc.

However, there is a way to objectivise these subjective experiences. The Holmes-Rahe Stress Inventory [1] is a scale rating life events according to the amount of stress they usually cause. The calculated score is a predictor of a chance of a major health breakdown in the next 2 years.

Stress can both boost and reduce our ability to learn, remember and also concentrate on the job at hand. In the extreme situations, stress can literally kill your brain connections, and as a result, significantly affect your cognitive performance.

Let's look at those scenarios now.

STRESS THAT BOOSTS YOUR COGNITIVE POWERS

So what makes a stressful experience a positive, focus-boosting one, and what makes it a negative, focus-damaging one?

(A little theory, which you can skip)

Any stressful event makes your hypothalamus—a part of your brain that is a sort of a control centre for the whole body—send signals that stimulate your adrenal glands to release so-called stress hormones. One of them is adrenaline—well-known for causing 'the adrenaline rush,' which not only speeds up your breathing and heartbeat, but also gives you a sense of increased strength and a sudden boost of energy.

Adrenaline makes you go into the 'fight or flight' response. This is exactly why this system evolved: to make us run away from the predator or fight for food or survival. Adrenaline helps us deal with stress quickly.

Cortisol is another hormone that helps us cope with highly stressful situations. It helps wipe out unpleasant effects of stress and enables your body to return to a baseline, normal state.

These reactions are manageable as long as the stress lasts only as long as running away from a sabre-toothed cat, or killing a mammoth. Unfortunately, in our modern lives, stressors are more likely to be of long-term duration. Working in a toxic place, living with chronic poor health, or trying to support yourself when studying full time may not be as stressful as putting your life on the line to fend off starvation, but it does not stop once the incident/event is over, and the effect of it extends and accumulates over time.

The power of so called Positive stress

You may have heard the term 'positive stress' (Eustress). Positive stress is the kind of stress that helps you mobilise yourself and use that adrenaline rush to progress. It's the way nature planned stress to be: speed up and get yourself away from the danger, or throw that stone harder and kill your dinner.

What makes stress positive/productive?

It's always individual, but as long as you perceive the situation as a challenge you are pursuing rather than an unwanted threat, you have a sense of control and meaning—you're onto it.

How to use (induce) the state of positive stress

When it comes to learning and other intellectual work requiring focus, there is a sweet spot called optimal emotional arousal—your body's emotional response to a situation. Too stressful (too much of a threat, too short a deadline, not enough money/expertise, etc.) and you will feel overwhelmed. Too long a period of stress and your recovery system will not cope.

If you can find that sweet spot of optimal emotional arousal—the 'not too much and not for too long'—you can use 'positive stress' to boost your ability to focus. Check Chapter 7 for some tips on how to use stress (and emotions) for better focus.

1. Stress that kills your cognitive powers

Sadly, it is not always possible to turn your stressful experience into positive, motivating stress. Situations that push us well out of our comfort zone, when we don't feel we have any control over it, or just stress that goes on for longer are particularly difficult. This is when stress is likely to kill your ability to focus, think, problem-solve, etc.

Unfortunately, chronic stress is something of a sign of our time. We may not need to go hunting for food or defend our lives on a regular basis, but living in overcrowded, noisy spaces, overwhelmed by technology, with too much choice and bombarded with bad news every day, is not all roses. The cult of super-productivity and pressure to succeed expressed in the number of overtime hours and extracurricular activities, and expectations to be 'always on/plugged-in,' add to the already long list of stressors.

Our internal stress management system is constantly working—dealing with the physiological effects of our hectic lives. And with our body flushed with stress hormones, our immune system gets depleted, our brain stops forming neural connections, some of the existing connections can be damaged, and in the most severe cases, stress can kill our brain cells.

In consequence, we get sick more often, our ability to remember things, plan, execute, calculate, etc., reduces, and our overall cognitive performance takes a plunge.

Chronic stress is one of the biggest enemies of your cognitive powers. Being able to effectively manage it is an essential skill necessary for high cognitive performance and ability to focus.

HOW TO MINIMISE THE NEGATIVE IMPACT OF STRESS ON YOUR ABILITY TO FOCUS

**Disclaimer: While the stress management techniques in this article can have a positive effect on reducing stress, they are for your information and educational purposes only. You should take the advice of a suitably qualified health professional if you have any concerns over stress-related illnesses, or if you are experiencing significant or persistent stress, anxiety, unhappiness or any other physical or mental health problems. **

Stress management has almost become a discipline in itself. There is lots of information out there, too much to include in this short book. For the purpose of this chapter, I will just concentrate on a few strategies that can be particularly useful in terms of improving your ability to focus, and easy enough to be implemented in your busy schedule.

Overall, there are two approaches to dealing with stress: change (avoid or alter) the stressful situation, or change the way we react to the stressor (adapt or accept).

I. Avoid or alter your situation to prevent stress

Know yourself, know your enemy

Identify what stresses you most often and explore the reasons why. Remember the old adage? The better you know your enemy, the better you can fight it. Some recommend a stress diary/journal where you would record what caused you to feel stressed, how it made you feel, what you did in response, and what was the result of your actions. This is as a method to help identify causes of stress and what helps or doesn't help in dealing with it.

Eliminate or reduce it

If, among your stressors, you find things that are not essential for your survival, explore whether you can eliminate or reduce the frequency or intensity of those events.

I accepted that driving is a big stressor of mine a long time ago. I've dumped all attempts to become a better driver—it was just not worth it. I've minimised the need to sit behind the wheel as much as I can (I use public transport and walk whenever I can; I also got quite relaxed about asking family, friends and colleagues for a lift, if possible). I also reduce the impact of it if I have to drive; for instance, choosing to do my weekly shopping in the early hours of Saturday or Sunday morning, when there is very little traffic, and the shop is empty (and this way I also reduce the stress of shopping!).

Get prepared

One of the most common causes of stress, particularly in educational and office work environments, is stress related to situations where you are assessed, judged or graded. So exams, assignments, presentations. There are many factors at play here, and I'd suggest you do some exploration to diagnose your own 'favourites.'

I have listed the most common scenarios and some suggestions for addressing the problem below.

- The actual level of skill and knowledge:
  If you think you don't know enough, make sure you address the skills or knowledge gap. Learn, prepare your presentation, revise, practice, rehearse. Practice in an environment similar to the stressful situation, so your retrieval can match the learning situation as much as possible.

- The performance itself:
  If you have issues performing, such as fear of speaking in public, or presenting in front of others, there are techniques designed for helping you deal with that. At the very extreme, fear of performance takes the shape of social anxiety and is a clinical problem that needs a specialist approach.

- The fear of failure:
  This is a common cause of stress and avoidance, and a complex one, too. To some extent, the fear of failure can be a motivator and a powerful driver of success. But too much of it is likely to make things worse, damaging not only to the outcomes of your work, but also your self-esteem and confidence.
  If your fear of failure is crushing your cognitive performance, here is what you can do:

  o Get prepared as well as you can, just as discussed above
  Analyse what may possibly go wrong and failure-proof your work to reduce the risk of it, e.g., if you are getting stressed about an exam or a deadline for a project report, on further exploration you're likely to find the following elements to your stress:
  o Actually failing to solve the exam problems/write the report (and hence a skill/knowledge gap, which you can close)
  o Not having enough time to complete all the problems/write the report (which can be addressed by starting earlier, planning it, managing your time actively)
  o Being late for the exam/presentation of the report (make sure you aren't)
  o Having a headache on the morning of the exam, etc. (have a packet of pain killers in your bag)

TIME STRESS

Pressures of time, deadlines, and juggling numerous commitments at the same time are the most common types of stress these days. They have a certain appeal and can be motivating (see the section on Positive Stress), but in moderation. To prevent time stress from affecting your ability to focus and think, take charge of your time through time management, planning, scheduling, etc.

The key to success is actually understanding what the elements of your stress are so you can deal with it appropriately; it really boils down to 'Know thyself and know thy enemy.'

- Be informed
  One of the reasons we find various situations or events stressful is because we can't see it coming. It works as a surprise, but an unpleasant one. Your account went into overdraft, or worse, you got a bailiff's letter because you weren't paying your mortgage? It's hardly an overnight thing, you should have seen it, if you'd kept an eye on your finance.
  The same goes for relationship trouble. Divorces or split-ups rarely happen without any warning.
  Don't hide your head in the sand. Be tuned to whatever is going on in your life. Keep your eyes, ears and other senses open to spot problems in the making to prevent them if you can.

- Don't overcommit
  Over commitment is another common reason we get stressed. Know your limits and learn to say NO.

- Don't get stressed over being stressed.
  Don't make your internal stress management system work any harder by stressing over being stressed. Accept that stress is part of our lives, learn to deal with it and move on.

2. ADAPT OR ACCEPT—LEARN TO DEAL WITH STRESS

It would be great if we could eliminate or avoid stress completely, but it's unrealistic. Stress is part of everyday life, and sometimes we just cannot avoid it.

There are lots of strategies for dealing with stress, but I will focus only on a few that I believe may help your cognitive performance. If you need more information, search the Internet or your local library. It is also important to remember that you should seek advice from your health professional if you are not coping well with stress or feeling down, unhappy. If you are feeling suicidal—contact your doctor immediately. This is for your information only, and you should execute your judgment before putting these strategies into practice, and always seek professional advice when necessary.

Here are a few strategies for managing stress:

- Make sure you are getting enough sleep and down-time. Sleep helps manage stress and boosts your cognitive powers. See Chapter 6 for more tips on how to sleep well

- Set aside relaxation/down-time and make sure you use it for exactly that—no cheating and doing more work. You may also want to explore the approach to energy management described in Chapter 11.

- Take regular breaks:
  Include short and longer breaks in your work/study day in the short and long run. If you can, try to avoid work/studying on weekends and evenings.
  Turn off your phone, don't check your emails, and make sure you have something nice planned.

- Develop a range of down-time strategies—make sure you include stuff you actually enjoy doing. It's good to involve some sensory experiences, like aromatherapy, listening to your favourite music, etc.

- Connect with friends and family, don't hesitate to ask them for help or support.
- Meditation/relaxation—another technique that should already be in your diary. If you remember well, meditation/relaxation is great for helping you sleep better; it is also a way of managing your emotions, so if you are not doing it already, it is time to consider including relaxation/meditation into your schedule.
- Have a healthy lifestyle:
  Exercise lovers (and haters), here is another piece of good news; exercise is not only great for your learning brain, and for your sleep, but also as a stress management technique. By including regular exercise into your routine you can kill three birds with one stone.
  Also, look at eliminating or reducing your amount of caffeine, sugar, and nicotine, avoid alcohol or drugs, eat a healthy diet.
- Acceptance
  Acceptance is another great way of managing stress in our life. For example, acceptance that stress is part of our life or that sometimes there are things we cannot change.

Hopefully, this chapter was not too stressful—just right on that sweet spot to motivate you to keep going. Now that you know how stress affects your focus and how to manage it, you can relax.

This chapter ends Part 3 of this book. I trust that you have a better understanding of typical focus problems and how to address them.

You are now ready to take action. Turn the page to see how to set up a system that will enable you to have your focus on an autopilot.

PART 4 -

TIME TO TAKE ACTION

CHAPTER 13 -
CREATE A LASER-SHARP
FOCUS SYSTEM

You are still with me—that's great. Thank you for carrying on with this journey.

You now know how to turn on your laser-sharp focus. That's great.

But your journey is not finished yet. Like any new skills, your ability to concentrate on the job at hand when you want it, for however long you want it, will need time to develop and strengthen.

So bear with it. Keep going. Don't give up if you don't get it right the first, second and even 55th time.

Keep trying. The more you try, the better you're going to get.

> *"The drops of rain make a hole in the stone, not by violence, but by oft falling."*
> *[Lucretius]*

An even more powerful way to develop 'a focus on autopilot' is to set up a system that will help you focus. Every. Single. Time.

How?

By creating a focus habit(s).

Habits—breaking bad ones and developing good ones—have been widely present in the media, particularly social media, over the last years. A quick Google search on habits in January 2015 returned 176 million webpages, not much less than searching for Justin Bieber (206 million) or Kim Kardashian (193 million). Why?

Studies show that over 40% of our lives is run by habits. [1] Yes, 40% of what we do every day is on automatic pilot.

Our life is a sum of habits.

A lot of things in our lives depend on our habits: healthy teeth—it's daily brushing, flossing and regular check-ups. Healthy heart: healthy diet, exercise, stress management. Being able to earn our living: getting up in the morning, getting ready for work and getting to work on time. Getting good grades: studying regularly, attending lectures and tutorials, being on time with your assignments and other things.

Our health, wealth, happiness, fitness and success depend on our habits.

Habits can help or destroy our goals, dreams, lives.

To manage distraction, avoid interruptions, get rid of procrastination and take control of technology for good, you need a truly long-term approach. The best way to develop a long-term approach is through building habits. Habits take the pressure off your willpower and motivation by creating an autopilot response.

"It's all good, Joanna," you may say. "But how do I do it?"

I. Master the Habit Loop

Every habit, good or bad, is developed and maintained in the same way.

An event, situation, smell, sound, etc., pops up and attracts our attention (the cue or trigger). As a response, we carry out a specific behaviour (the routine), which provides us with a reward.

The Cue/Trigger—Routine—Reward loop is called **The Habit Loop** and lies at the heart of every behaviour on autopilot. Every time you preform your habitual behaviour, you are rewarded, and that's why you keep coming back for more. The longer you perform this sequence, the stronger the habit is engrained in your brain. Because, yes, our habits are 'encoded' in our neural pathways.

A lot has been said and written about developing and changing habits. The key to a successful habit development is nailing down the habit loop:

The Habit Loop

Start by identifying what new behaviour you want to implement. Then choose a trigger (cue) and your reward. Keep practicing.

My morning routine is based on a number of little daily habits. While the first 45 minutes of the day is 'me time' when I can just enjoy my coffee and breakfast while checking my emails and social media, when the clock strikes 6, a more serious work begin.

I have set up my iCal reminders for any planned work at 6 a.m. When the message pops up, it's a signal for me to get down to work—this is my Trigger.

Once I complete my morning tasks (Behaviour), I get a little break to get another cup of coffee (Reward).

2. Tweak the process along the way (until it works every time)

Experiment with various triggers. I described a time-based trigger above. Time-based triggers are good, but may not work for everyone in every situation, and are pretty rigid. If you need more flexibility, choose an activity-based trigger, e.g., you start working on your tasks after you've had your coffee or when you put your 'writing hat' on (sounds silly, but I know people for whom this silly trick works wonders).

The easiest way to find a trigger is to use something you already do on regular basis, e.g. drinking your morning cup of coffee, brushing your teeth, or getting dressed. This way, you don't have to worry about forgetting your trigger.

3. Nail down your Reward system

The key to successful habits is a good rewarding system, because it's the reward that keep your habit loop going. Make sure you choose a reward that you really care about. Don't overuse extrinsic rewards.

For more tips on rewards, check Chapter 4.

4. Practice, practice, practice

The more you practice the new behaviour, the closer you get to developing a habit. It's not just the good old 'practice makes perfect' that is at work here, but also the habit loop and its neural pathway in our brain that becomes reinforced.

Accept that it will take time to put your new behaviour on autopilot. How long? It's individual and depends on a variety of factors, i.e., the complexity of the new habit and how rewarding you find it (that's why it's really important to get the reward right). Studies showed that on average it takes 66 days, but the length of time can range from 18 to 254 days.

To keep going, focus on practice rather than performance. Don't worry about mastery—make sure you carry out the behaviour every time you experience the trigger.

Assume you will fall off track and plan for it. Get back on track as soon as you can.

Monitor your progress—it helps with motivation and reinforces the habit cycle as the behaviour becomes automatic.

5. FOCUS ON ONE LITTLE CHANGE AT THE TIME

Behaviour change is hard. Anyone who has tried dieting, quitting smoking or even exercising more can testify to that.

We are creatures of habits, which means once something becomes a habit, it is hard to get rid of it.

And if you ever tried to change more than one thing at a time, like me trying to eat fewer sweets and exercise regularly, you know how much harder this is.

> *"Commit to one goal for an extended period of time, and make sure all other goals are secondary or nonexistent for the time being. Give yourself grace in the other areas and focus all of your attention on improving in this one, specific area."*
>
> S. J. Scott: *77 Good Habits to Live A Better Life* [2]

Focusing on one little change at the time is a powerful strategy. Choose one simple action that can be completed in a few minutes first, and practice it until you have it on autopilot.

For instance, to master your environment, start scanning your environment for anything that can distract you before you sit at your desk.

Find a cue (for me, it's the moment I open my laptop—I pause to take a look around and eliminate anything that can distract or interrupt me). Think of the reward.

Don't move to the next step until you perform this action every time you sit at your desk to focus on your job.

Once you've got it nailed down, expand to the next little step. For example, it may be rearranging stuff on your desk so that you only have what you need in your Optimal Viewing and Normal Reach zones. Again—find a Cue, set up a reward (for practical purposes this may be the same reward you have for the previous action).

Keep going until you do it automatically.

S. J. Scott, the author of several books on habits and blogger from DevelopGoodHabits.Com has come up with the idea of habit stacking: adding little changes to your behaviour, one after another, to build a ritual that you follow on a daily basis. Habit stacking eliminates the stress of having to remember it all at once, and the pressure on your willpower and motivation. You change your behaviour one little step at a time.

This is how I built my powerful morning routine many years ago, even though I was completely oblivious to the science of developing habits: taking one little change at a time and mastering it. More recently, I've started changing my evening routine, adding yoga/Pilates and regular reading time.

The effects of stacking habits are powerful. It is definitely one of the ways you can develop a system for a focus on autopilot. You can read more about it in S.J.'s book: *Habit Stacking. 97 Small Life Changes That Can Take 5 Minutes or Less*

6. PUT IT ON A CHECKLIST

An excellent way to boost your ability to complete these actions is through writing your routines down in the form of a checklist. Every time your trigger cues you, you go through the steps as described on your checklist. S.J. Scott recommends checklists for his habit stacking approach as well. It's an easy way to remember what you are supposed to do and to keep yourself on track.

Create your own checklist, including steps you want to take when addressing various elements of your focus system, e.g., for scanning your environment you can write the following steps/checks:

- Chair ready?
- Optimal Viewing Zone, only with necessary stuff?
- Normal Reach Zone cleared of clutter?

- Notifications off?
- Etc.

Need more help in setting up a laser-sharp focus on autopilot system?

If you're interested in learning how to implement a laser-sharp focus on autopilot, keep in touch. I am working on adding a special program to help you master it faster.

Stay in touch. If you haven't yet, subscribe to my mailing list for updates and more tips and tricks to speed up your learning and personal change.

Visit: www.shapeshiftersclub.com to subscribe.

To Your Success. Faster.

Joanna Jast

BONUSES

To download all your bonuses, go to:
http://www.theshapeshiftersclub.com/lsf-reader-bonus/ and use "LSF
reader" as the password.

DID YOU ENJOY LASER-SHARP FOCUS?

First of all, let me thank you for choosing this book from many others on the same topic. Thank you for giving me a chance and thank you for reading the book to the very end.

If you liked my book and want to help others, and me, here is how you can do it.

Spread the word. Write a review. Let others know what you liked about my book, how it helped you get better at what you do or how it thought you to do it faster.

It doesn't have to be a long review—a few lines would be great.

Reviews help authors continue writing books that help people like you get results they want.

Reviews help people like you choose books that will help them get results they want.

And if you loved the book, let me know. You can email me at joanna@shapeshiftersclub.com, connect with me on Twitter: @ShapeShift_Club and Facbook: Shapeshifters Club.

RESOURCES AND FURTHER READING

Here is a list of resources I used when researching this book.

INTRODUCTION

(1) American Psychological Association. 2006. "Multitasking: Switching Costs."
Accessed at: http://www.apa.org/research/action/multitask.aspx

CHAPTER 1

(1) Castle P, Buckler S. 2009. "What Was I Saying? Concentration and Attention in How to Be a Successful Teacher."
Accessed on 11 November 2015 at:
http://www.sagepub.com/sites/default/files/upm-binaries/28824_02_Castle_&_Buckler_Ch_02.pdf.

(2) Medina J. 2011. "Brain Rules: 12 Principles for Surviving and Thriving at Work, Home and School." Kindle Edition.

CHAPTER 2

(1) Saber Teheran AS, Lee H et al. 2013. "25-Year Summary of US Malpractice Claims for Diagnostic Errors 1986-2010: An Analysis from the

National Practitioner Data Bank." *BMJ Quality & Safety*.
Accessed on 11 November 2015 at:
http://www.ncbi.nlm.nih.gov/pubmed/23610443.

CHAPTER 3

(1) HILT (Harvard Initiative for Learning and Teaching): "Setting Goals: Who, Why, How?"
Accessed at: http://hilt.harvard.edu/files/hilt/files/settinggoals.pdf.

(2) Gomez-Minambres J. 2012. "Motivation Through Goal Setting." *Journal of Economic Psychology*, vol 33 (6), December 2012
Accessed at: http://www.researchgate.net/profile/Joaquin_Gomez-Minambres/publication/261862145_Motivation_through_goal_setting/links/0f317536005cd902a0000000.pdf.

(3) Martin, L.L. & Tesser A. 2014. "Striving and Feeling: Interactions Among Goals, Affect, and Self-Regulation." New York/East Sussex. Psychology Press.

(4) Taing M.U., Smith, T. Et al. 2013. "The Relationship Between Learning Goal Orientation, Goal Setting, and Performance: A Longitudinal Study." *Journal of Applied Social Psychology*, 43, pp. 1668-1675.

(5) Csikszentmihalyi M. 1990. Flow: "The Psychology of Optimal Experience." Harper Collins.

(6) Gollwitzer P.M. & Sheehan P. 2006. Implementation Intentions and Goal Achievement: A Meta-Analysis of Effects and Processes. *Advances in Experimental Social Psychology*. Vol 38.
Accessed at:
http://www.sciencedirect.com/science/article/pii/S0065260106380021

(7) Scott Dinsmore: "Warren Buffet's 5-Step Process for Prioritising True Success and Why Most People Never Do It." *Live Your Legend*
Accessed at: http://liveyourlegend.net/warren-buffetts-5-step-process-for-prioritizing-true-success-and-why-most-people-never-do-it/

Chapter 4

(1) Clear, James. "Achieve Your Goals: Research Reveals a Simple Trick That Doubles Your Chances for Success."
Accessed at: http://jamesclear.com/implementation-intentions?

(2) Statistic Brain Research Institute. 2015. "New Year's Resolution Statistics."
Accessed at: http://www.statisticbrain.com/new-years-resolution-statistics/

(3) Pink, Daniel H. 2010. "Drive: The Surprising Truth About What Motivates Us." (Kindle edition)

Chapter 5

(1) Abadie A., Gay S. 2005. "The Impact of Presumed Consent Legislation on Cadaveric Organ Donation: A Cross Country Study"
Accessed at: http://www.hks.harvard.edu/fs/aabadie/pconsent.pdf

(2) Smith A. 1989. "A Review of the Effects of Noise on Human Performance." *Scandinavian Journal of Psychology*, vol 30(3). P. 185-206.
Accessed at: http://onlinelibrary.wiley.com/doi/10.1111/j.1467-9450.1989.tb01082.x/abstract

(3) Szalma, J L.; Hancock, P. A. 2011. "Noise Effects on Human Performance: A Meta-Analytic Synthesis." *Psychological Bulletin*, Vol 137(4), Jul 2011, 682-707.
Accessed at: http://psycnet.apa.org/journals/bul/137/4/682/

(4) Bowman K. (2015). "Don't Just Sit There." Priopiometrics Press

Chapter 6

(1) National Sleep Foundation. "How Much Sleep Do We Really Need?"
Accessed at: https://sleepfoundation.org/how-sleep-works/how-much-sleep-do-we-really-need

(2) Soong, Jennifer. "The Secret (and Surprising) Power of Naps." WebMD Magazine.

Accessed at: http://www.webmd.com/balance/features/the-secret-and-surprising-power-of-naps.

(3) National Sleep Foundation: "Ask The Expert—Sleep Hygiene."
Accessed at: http://sleepfoundation.org/ask-the-expert/sleep-hygiene)

(4) Kleitman N. 1963. "Sleep and Wakefulness." University of Chicago Press (1987 reprint)

(5) Schwartz T: "The 90-Minute Solution: How Building in Periods of Renewal Can Change Your Work and Your Life. *HuffPost Healthy Living*.
Accessed at: http://www.huffingtonpost.com/tony-schwartz/work-life-balance-the-90_b_578671.html

(6) Berg JM, Tymoczko JL, and Stryer L. (2002). "Each Organ Has a Unique Metabolic Profile." *In Biochemistry. 5th edition.*
Accessed at: http://www.ncbi.nlm.nih.gov/books/NBK22436/

(7) Medina J. 2011. "Brain Rules: 12 Principles for Surviving and Thriving at Work, Home and School." Kindle Edition.

(8) Medina J. "Brain Rules"
Accessed at: http://www.brainrules.net/exercise

(9) Cappelletti S., et al. 2015. "Caffeine: Cognitive and Physical Performance Enhancer or Psychoactive Drug? *Current Neuropharmacology, 13(1)*.
Accessed at: http://www.ncbi.nlm.nih.gov/pmc/articles/PMC4462044/

(10) Persad LAB. 2011. "Energy drinks and the Neurophysiological Impact of Caffeine." *Front Neuroscience*, 5: 116.
Accessed at: http://www.ncbi.nlm.nih.gov/pmc/articles/PMC3198027/

(11) Stirley CW, Khan SR. 2014. "Review of the energy drink literature from 2013: findings continue to support most risk from mixing with alcohol".
Current Opinions in Psychiatry, 27(4)
Accessed at: http://www.ncbi.nlm.nih.gov/pubmed/24852059

(12) Ibrahim NK, Iftikhar R. 2014. "Energy drinks: Getting wings but at what health cost" *Pakistan Journal of Medical Sciences*, 30(6)
Accessed at: http://www.ncbi.nlm.nih.gov/pmc/articles/PMC4320741/

Also websites:

Mayo Clinic: www.mayoclinic.org,
NHS (National Health Service) Choices. Health A-Z: www.nhs.uk,
WebMD: www.webmd.com,
Harvard School of Public Health: http://www.hsph.harvard.edu

CHAPTER 7

(1) Grossman P, Riemann L., et al. 2004. "Mindfulness-Based Stress Reduction and Health Benefits: A Meta-Analysis." *Journal of Psychosomatic Research*, vol 57(1).
Accessed at:
http://www.sciencedirect.com/science/article/pii/S0022399903005737

(2) Allen D. 2002. "Getting Things Done: The Art of Stress-Free Productivity." Kindle edition.

(3) Van Raalte, J L., Brewer, B W., et al. 1994. "The Relationship Between Observable Self-Talk and Competitive Junior Tennis Players' Match Performances." *Journal of Sport & Exercise Psychology*, Vol 16(4)
Accessed at: http://psycnet.apa.org/psycinfo/1995-24711-001

(4) Hamilton, R.A., Scott D., and McDougall, M.P. 2007. "Assessing the Effectiveness of Self-Talk Interventions on Endurance Performance. *Journal of Applied Sport Psychology*, Vol 19(2).
Accessed at:
http://www.tandfonline.com/doi/abs/10.1080/10413200701230613

Also:

Barker J. "Express Yourself: Your Mouth, Your Life. Turn Down Negative Self-Talk." WebMD.
Accessed at: http://www.webmd.com/balance/express-yourself-13/negative-self-talk

CHAPTER 8

(1) Steel, P. 2007. "The Nature of Procrastination: A Meta-Analytic and Theoretical Review of Quintessential Self-Regulatory Failure." *Psychological Bulletin*, 133(1)
Accessed at:
http://dspace.ucalgary.ca/jspui/bitstream/1880/47914/1/Steel_PsychBull etin_2007_Postprint.pdf.

(2) The Pomodoro Technique: http://pomodorotechnique.com/

(3) Newport, C. 2008. "Fixed-Schedule Productivity: How I Accomplish a Large Amount of Work In a Small Number of Work Hours."
Accessed at: http://calnewport.com/blog/2008/02/15/fixed-schedule-productivity-how-i-accomplish-a-large-amount-of-work-in-a-small-number-of-work-hours/

CHAPTER 9

No specific references to note

CHAPTER 10

(1) American Psychological Association. 2006. "Multitasking: Switching Costs."
Accessed at: http://www.apa.org/research/action/multitask.aspx

(2) Monsell, S. 2003. "Task Switching." *TRENDS in Cognitive Science*, Vol 7(3)
Accessed at:
http://psychology.illinoisstate.edu/cbs/readings/Monsell_(2003).pdf

(3) Schaffer, O. 2013. "Crafting Fun User Experiences: A Method to Facilitate Flow."
Accessed at: http://humanfactors.com/whitepapers/crafting_fun_ux.asp

(4) Csikszentmihalyi, M.1990. "Flow: The Psychology of Optimal Experience." Harper Collins.

(5) Medina, J. 2011. "Brain Rules: 12 Principles for Surviving and Thriving at Work, Home and School." Kindle Edition.

CHAPTER 11

(1) http://www.merriam-webster.com/dictionary/energy

(2) http://theenergyproject.com/eu/key-ideas

(3) Oswald, A.J., Proto, E., and Sgroi, D. 2014. "Happiness and Productivity." *JOLE* 3rd Version.
Accessed at:
http://www2.warwick.ac.uk/fac/soc/economics/staff/eproto/workingpapers/happinessproductivity.pdf.

(4) Schwartz, T. 2013. "Relax! You'll Be More Productive." *The New York Times*
Accessed at:
http://www.nytimes.com/2013/02/10/opinion/sunday/relax-youll-be-more-productive.html

(5) Alhola, P., Polo-Kantola, P. 2007. "Sleep Deprivation: Impact on Cognitive Performance." *Neuropsychiatric Disease and Treatment* 3(5): 553-567.
Accessed at: http://www.ncbi.nlm.nih.gov/pmc/articles/PMC2656292/

(6) Fritz, C., Sonnentag, S. 2006. "Recovery, Well-Being and Performance-Related Outcomes: The Role of Workload and Vacation Experiences." *Journal of Applied Psychology*, 91(4): 936-45.
Accessed at: http://www.ncbi.nlm.nih.gov/pubmed/16834516

(7) Barker, E. 2012. "Happy Thoughts: Here Are the Things Proven to Make You Happy."
Accessed at: http://www.bakadesuyo.com/2012/08/here-are-the-things-that-are-proven-to-make-y/

(8) Association for Psychological Science. 2012. "More Than Just Zoning Out—Psychological Science Examines Cognitive Process Underlying Mind Wandering."
Accessed at:

http://www.psychologicalscience.org/index.php/news/releases/more-than-just-zoning-out-psychological-science-examines-the-cognitive-processes-underlying-mind-wandering.html.

(9) National Sleep Foundation: "How Much Sleep Do You Need?"
Accessed at: http://sleepfoundation.org/how-sleep-works/how-much-sleep-do-we-really-need/page/0/1

(10) Lyubomirsky, S., et al. 2005. "Pursuing Happiness: The Architecture of Sustainable Change." *Review of General Psychology*, Vol 9(2), 111-131.
Accessed at: http://psycnet.apa.org/psycinfo/2005-06355-003/

(11) Sheldon, K.M., Lyubomirsky, S. 2006. "How to Increase and Sustain Positive Emotion: The Effects of Expressing Gratitude and Visualizing Best Possible Selves." *The Journal of Positive Psychology*, vol 1(2)
Accessed at:
http://www.tandfonline.com/doi/abs/10.1080/17439760500510676

Also:
https://en.wikipedia.org/wiki/Sleep_deprivation
https://en.wikipedia.org/wiki/Maslow%27s_hierarchy_of_needs

CHAPTER 12

(1) Holmes-Rahe Stress Inventory:
Accessed at: http://www.stress.org/holmes-rahe-stress-inventory/

(2) Medina, J. 2011. "Brain Rules: 12 Principles for Surviving and Thriving at Work, Home and School." Kindle Edition.

(3) McIntyre, C.K., Roozendaal, B. 2007. "Adrenal Stress Hormones and Enhanced Memory for Emotionally Arousing Experiences." *Neural Plasticity and Memory: From Genes to Brain Imaging*.
Accessed at: http://www.ncbi.nlm.nih.gov/books/NBK3907/

Also:
http://www.nhs.uk/conditions/stress-anxiety-depression/pages/understanding-stress.aspx
http://www.nhs.uk/Conditions/stress-anxiety-depression/Pages/reduce-

stress.aspx

http://www.apa.org/helpcenter/stress.aspx

http://www.apa.org/helpcenter/chronic-stress.aspx

CHAPTER 13

(1) Duhigg, C. 2012. "The Power of Habits: Why We Do What We Do and How to Change." Kindle Edition.

(2) Scott, S.J. "77 Good Habits to Live A Better Life." Accessed at: http://www.developgoodhabits.com

(3) Scott, S.J. 2014. "97 Small Life Changes That Can Take 5 Minutes or Less." Kindle Edition.

ABOUT THE AUTHOR

Joanna Jast is a mid-life career shifter helping people who, like her, need to adapt to new environments, jobs, lives, through fast learning and personal change using evidence-based and well-proven methods.

Trained as a doctor, Joanna has always kept her interests wide. She has always been in more than one job, studying part time, volunteering, learning and teaching languages, writing, and having a life at the same time. With this level of busyness, she had to develop a good system to keep herself on track, on time, and on budget.

Her love for productivity, effectiveness and top-notch mental powers combined with her low threshold for boredom resulted in a passion for finding shortcuts and well-proven strategies that work.

This book is a result of years of experience as a student, employee, freelancer, entrepreneur and teacher. The strategies and tricks described in it helped Joanna get through her medical training unscathed (and even with good grades), get a few more qualifications along the way (including an MBA), master two foreign languages, write two non-fiction books and a couple of novels, climb the corporate ladder (and then jump off it), and survive a few entrepreneurial attempts, while still being a (reasonably) sane mother, wife and friend.

She is currently on a mission to help people tired of padded-out, wishy-washy, heavy on marketing and light on evidence self-help advice accelerate their learning and personal change. If you want access to more practical, actionable and tried and tested advice on speeding up your success, and/or would like to find out more about her, visit: www.shapeshiftersclub.com

To Your Success. Faster.

Made in the USA
Middletown, DE
29 November 2017